DATE DUE

MAR 06	APR 6 '94	
MAY 8		
MAR 26 '75		
APR 30 '7		
MAY 21		
JUN 7 '75		
OCT 15 '7		
JUN 2 '76		
NOV 23 '77		
DEC 2 '80		
FEB 23 '94		
MAR 9 '94		

TEPOZTLAN
A MEXICAN VILLAGE

TEPOZTLAN
A MEXICAN VILLAGE

A Study of Folk Life

By ROBERT REDFIELD

THE UNIVERSITY OF CHICAGO PRESS

CHICAGO & LONDON

Library of Congress Catalog Card Number: 30-15556

THE UNIVERSITY OF CHICAGO PRESS, CHICAGO 60637
The University of Chicago Press, Ltd., London W. C. 1

PREFACE

The materials embodied in this volume were collected by the writer from November, 1926, to July, 1927. They are no more than a small sample of materials which might be obtained. They are far from constituting an ethnographic monograph on the people of Tepoztlán. Eight months is too short a time within which to secure the data for such a monograph. One would have to spend a considerably longer period, and one would need a command of both languages spoken in the community, not merely a fair knowledge of one of them. Eight months is not even time enough to correct all one's initial blunders. That this report still contains some positive mistakes the writer knows is likely. The materials are now published only because it seems improbable that he will soon be able to return to Tepoztlán to continue the study here only introduced. In order to indicate some of the limitations of the materials, statements derived, not from the direct observation of the flow of custom in the village, but from accounts, insufficiently corroborated, of informants, are so indicated in footnotes.

The study was initiated under the encouragement and direction of Dr. Fay-Cooper Cole, and was made possible by a fellowship granted by the Social Science Research Council. The writer has had much opportunity to learn from Dr. Robert E. Park, and has likewise received stimulus and suggestion from Dr. Edward Sapir. In Mexico, Dr. Manuel Gamio extended invaluable advice and practical aid. Acknowledgment is also to be made of the courteous assistance of Dr. J. Reygadas Vértiz. Señorita Elena Landazuri helped largely in recording musical notation. A small part of the help received from Margaret Park Redfield, both in collecting and presenting materials, is specifically acknowledged in the following pages. Finally, the writer feels a great obligation to the Tepoztecans themselves, whose friendly co-operation made this stay pleasant and showed the possibility of some day making an intensive study of Tepoztlán. Many names might be mentioned, but particularly those of Don Cruz Villamil, *barrio* of Santa Cruz; Doña Soledad Villamil, *barrio* of Santa Cruz; Don Jesús Balderrama, *barrio* of Santo Domingo; Don Ignacio Cortez, *barrio* of San Sebastian; Don Gilberto Gaillardo, *barrio* of San Miguel; and, most especially, Don Jesús Condé, *barrio* of San Miguel.

Chapters ii and iv have already appeared, in a somewhat different form, in the *American Anthropologist*.

ROBERT REDFIELD

TABLE OF CONTENTS

LIST OF ILLUSTRATIONS
FOLLOWING PAGE 120

viii

INTRODUCTION: THE MEXICAN FOLK

The terms "folk lore," "folk song," and even "folk ways" have a meaning in considering Mexico which they lack in connection with a country such as ours. The ways of the folk, largely unwritten and unremarked, constitute the real Mexico. "In few countries," says Gruening, "is political history less significant than in Mexico, yet its historiographies are pre-eminently political."[1] The formal institution, the explicit statement of program or policy, the bulk of contemporary documents, lie remote from the ways of the masses and record their history almost not at all. The world of the cultivated classes, who alone are articulate and who alone communicate freely with us, is a world apart from that of the folk. To learn and to set down the ways of the folk, one must encounter them directly and intimately; they are not otherwise to be found. Ethnology is the form which any careful study of contemporary history tends to take in Mexico.

I

What is the "folk"? If its meaning be reached backward from the terms which begin this page, it is a group which has folk lore and folk songs. For such material the collector goes to the primitive tribes or to the simpler peasant peoples enclaved within the

[1] Ernest Gruening, *Mexico and Its Heritage*, page x.

borders of civilized nations. These are "folk" peoples.
What characteristics distinguish them? Such peoples
enjoy a common stock of tradition; they are the car-
riers of a culture. This culture preserves its continuity
from generation to generation without depending upon
the printed page. Moreover, such a culture is local;
the folk has a habitat. Wandering folk, as, for example, the gypsy, do occur, but then special factors of
social isolation cause them to preserve their folk character among a people who are not folk. Within the
folk group there is relatively small diversity of intellectual interest; attitudes and interests are much the
same from individual to individual, although, presumably, there is the same range of inherent temperament
as in any other group of the same size. And finally, the
folk peoples are country peoples. If folk lore is encountered in the cities it is never in a robust condition,
but always diminishing, always a vestige.

There are plenty of such folk peoples in Mexico.
Some, like the Lacandones and (until perhaps recently) the Tarahumares, are as truly primitive, as truly
preliterate, as a Melanesian tribe. More, however,
have long since reached an adjustment with Western
civilization, as represented by the upper and govern-
ing classes; and now the complex of their culture is interwoven with the modern social and economic order.
They use money, wear commercial textiles, perhaps
know how to read and write, and employ at least the
terminology and some of the ritual forms of Catholic
Christianity. They are much like isolated, illiterate

peasant peoples everywhere. The former class of peoples have been regarded as the subject of ethnology (*Völkerkunde*); the second of what has conventionally been distinguished as "folk lore" (*Volkskunde*). Both sorts of groups are folk peoples.

But the series of culture types to be found in Mexico does not end with these simple societies. Mexico is in no small part modern; every year it becomes more so. In the more sophisticated villages of the north, in the middle classes in the cities everywhere, are to be found a people much like the masses in our own country. They not only can read, but they do read. The folk hear rumor; these people read news. Through the newspaper and its closely related organs of information and popular interest, the popular magazine and the moving picture, these latter people come to share in interests which are not local but are even international. Communication by way of oral tradition with the preceding generations has with such people come to play a smaller part in determining the patterns of their thinking; they are communicating with contemporaries like themselves in other cities and in other lands; and through printing and pictures they draw upon the accumulated experience of groups geographically and historically remote. They are ceasing, or have already ceased, to be a folk people.

Apparently there are people in Mexico who are folk peoples, with folk lore and folk songs and folk ways which are often indigenous and local to the particular community, but there are also people, largely in the

towns, who are no more a folk people than are the
citizens of Grand Rapids or Bridgeport. And apparently the "modernization" of Mexico is the gain of
this second kind of people at the expense of the first.
Yet in spite of this change, the bulk of the Mexican
population are folk. With us it is the other way. The
southern negro is our one principal folk. He has a local
tradition orally transmitted; he makes folk songs. Except for him we have to search for folk peoples in the
United States. In the mountains of the South and
Southeast we have a sort of vestigial folk. And here
and there, in such occupations as involve long periods
of isolation and a relative independence of the printed
page—as, for example, among lumbermen or cowboys
—a sort of quasi-folk develop, who write anonymous
folk songs and sometimes build up, around campfires,
folk sagas of the Paul Bunyan variety.

II

How are we to define the difference between the
Mexican masses and our own? What are some of the
characteristics of the folk that set them off from "the
common people" who are not folk? It may be suggested that the difference is made clear in the distinction between folk song and popular song, folk tale
and popular literature. It is, at the extremes, the difference between the animal tales or witch stories of
tribal Indian or simple peasant, and the American
magazines of the "true confessions" type. Or it is the
difference between the traditional chant to accom-

pany Indian or African ritual, or the equally traditional folk song of Mexican *peón* or Roumanian peasant, and "Singin' in the Rain" or "You've Never Been
Blue."

It perhaps needs to be pointed out that these two
sorts of songs, two sorts of literatures, are alike at all.
But alike they certainly are. They belong together
when contrasted with the sophisticated art and literature of the more self-conscious intelligentsia. They are
quite different, and different in the same way, from
Proust or Stravinsky. They are both, folk song and
popular song, written because they will be sung; they
are both, folk tale and popular story, composed because they will be heard or read. The sophisticated
art is formed in conformity with self-conscious canons
of taste. It is composed not to be read by everybody,
but to be appreciated by the few. It is written not in
the widespread and easy images of the folk, but in
more deliberately constructed forms. It has a horror,
for example, of *clichés*.

This is the difference which Sumner[1] speaks of when

[1] "It is a question of the first importance for the historian whether the mores
of the historical classes of which he finds evidence in documentary remains pene-
trated the masses or not. The masses are the real bearers of the mores of the
society. They carry tradition. The folkways are their ways. They accept influence or leadership and they imitate, but they do so as they see fit, being controlled by their notions and tastes previously acquired. They may accept standards of character and action from the classes, or from foreigners, or from literature, or from a new religion, but whatever they take up they assimilate and make
it a part of their own mores, which they then transmit by tradition, defend in its
integrity, and refuse to discard again. Consequently the writings of the literary
class may not represent the faiths, notions, tastes, standards, etc., of the masses
at all. The literature of the first Christian centuries shows us scarcely anything of
the mores of the time, as they existed in the faith and practice of the masses.

he distinguishes the "masses" from the "classes." The "classes" are the minority of sophisticated people who at least in literate society tend to occupy a mental world apart from that of the masses. The "masses," on the other hand, include both "folk" peoples and the common people of civilized and completely literate countries. For this second kind of "masses" there appears to be no name available,[1] and inventing new terms is of doubtful wisdom. Completing the proportion: "folk" is to "folk song" as "popular song" is to x—one might suggest *populus*, or better, *demos*.

The differences between folk song and popular song, or folk tale and popular literature, afford an approach to the difference between "folk" and *demos*. The popular song is obviously more sophisticated. It is written deliberately, for sale. The folk song is more "artless." The popular song has an author; the folk song easily loses its composer. The question of communal composition does not arise in the realm of popular literature as distinguished from folk literature. The popular song or story is written in order that it may

---

Every group takes out of a new religion which is offered to it just what it can assimilate with its own traditional mores. Christianity was a very different thing amongst Jews, Egyptians, Greeks, Germans and Slavs. It would be a great mistake to suppose that any people ever accepted and held philosophical or religious teaching as it was offered to them, and as we find it recorded in the books of the teachers. The mores of the masses admit of no such sudden and massive modification by doctrinal teaching. The process of assimilation is slow, and is attended by modifying influences at every stage" (*Folkways*, p. 46).

Sumner did not distinguish between the folk, a country people among whom culture is built up, and the urban proletariat, among whom it tends to break down.

[1] "Proletariat" appears to be a related term.

be sold; the composer earns a living out of it, or hopes to. And finally, there is the obvious and important difference between a composition that depends upon writing and one that needs only singing or speaking and hearing. And from this difference flow a number of significant correlaries. The folk song is much more local; it is commonly expressed in local terms; it has local allusions. The popular song refers to a much wider community of experience. The popular song, being written, is standardized; of it one does not collect "versions." Popular songs that develop versions are passing into folk songs. But the *Saturday Evening Post* appears in almost three million identical versions every Thursday. And the popular song, the popular story, exist in the world of fashion and fad. Among the folk, where communication is much slower, there is much less fashion; at least, in folk literature, there are probably no "rages." The "rage" is a trait of the *demos*.

If we turn to the songs and to the literature which are current in Mexico, we find examples of all three sorts: sophisticated, popular, and folk. That type of song and story which has widest currency, however, is in many respects transitional between folk literature and popular literature, folk song and popular song. The more primitive village peoples still sing the ancient traditional songs and tell the old traditional tales. The peoples of the towns and cities, at least the middle and upper classes there, sing sentimental songs, which are locally Mexican, and even the jazz ditties of

ephemeral favor in New York or London. But in between lies a great mass of transitional literature, a
sort of "folk-popular" literature, which expresses the
fact that in Mexico we have a collection of folk peoples
who are becoming *demos*.

This intermediate literature is best known from its
outstanding form, the ballad known as *corrido*.[1] The
corrido is in first instance orally transmitted. The composer, a singer of local prestige, communicates it to
the circle of listeners; it tends immediately to become
anonymous. But it is not wholly independent of writing. In the rural districts it may be set down in private copy-books, and in the cities it sometimes circu-
lates on cheap printed leaflets—just as did the "broad-
side ballad" of Elizabethan England.

[1] "The commonest form of musical expression is the *corrido*, literally, 'current happening.' Any event that touches the people immediately finds its way
into this form of ballad. Its words are printed on a gaudy sheet of paper, usually
green or pink, embellished often by a lurid wood cut. The verse is doggerel and
the music a 'catchy' refrain. But the *corridos* are a valuable index to popular
thought. During the Revolution Zapata outranked all other figures in the variety
and number of *corridos* about him. Villa, pictured as 'muy hombre,' the hero of
gigantic exploits, came next. Carranza did not figure in *corridos*—he made no
appeal to popular imagination. 'The arm of Obregon'—the arm lost on the field
of battle—did. Heroic, tragic, gruesome, pathetic themes prevail. Deeds of val-
or, floods, earthquakes, famines, calamities generally, which affect the people, are
instantly sung. The writer usually begins by announcing the subject of his verse
—as if addressing an audience, and in concluding often takes leave of it. He is a
modern troubadour—but instead of offering his vocal wares to the mighty, as of
old, the people are his patrons, for the *corridos* are sold for a centavo or two in
the markets.

"An essential quality of the *corridos* is their ingenuousness: The writer is
wholly frank. He tells not only of his hero's prowess, but of his weaknesses—his
drunkenness, his offenses against law and order, his fickleness to his sweethearts,
as well as their faithlessness. And just as he views the hero of his theme without
illusion he applies similar measurements to the great and near-great of his country—the generals and politicians" (Gruening, *op. cit.*, pp. 647–48).

The subject matter of this popular literature is always what interests the Mexican masses: war, crime, catastrophe, and especially popular heroes and popular scapegoats. And in its constantly shifting content, as the old *corridos* die and the new *corridos* are composed, it constitutes a sort of collective diary of the Mexican masses. At its lower margin, in the more traditional songs that persist in local communities for generations, this literature merges with the typical folk literature of primitive peoples. Its upper margin, the news ballad of crime or passion, passes into the lower margin of our own popular literature—the doggerel verses about Floyd Collins or the Hall-Mills case now circulated on mail-order phonograph records.

The essential difference between the *corrido* and the folk song of a truly primitive people appears to lie in the tendency of the *corrido* to enter into the realm of news, public opinion, and even propaganda. The *corrido* is a news organ. It informs what comes to be a public of the events which concern it, and especially of the excitements which nourish its interest. It tends, one would venture, to become a mechanism for conflicting local attitudes. A man sung as a bandit in one community may be sung as a redeemer in another; the circulation of these songs tends to define his position in more generally accepted terms. In this relation of the *corrido* to a discussion which is more impersonal than the intimate interchange of ideas in a completely self-sufficient folk community, the *corrido* is related to that rise of nationalistic feeling which begins to give to the changes which are going on in Mexico a special, and at the same time a characteristic, form.

III

The change which is obviously going on in Mexico can be described, it may be, in terms more fundamental than "the spread of education" or "economic development," although these are of course important aspects of that change. To the social anthropologist the change is that which is represented by the gain of popular literature at the expense of folk literature. It is a change in type of culture. It may furthermore be provisionally assumed that this change has elements in common with others which are taking place in countries similarly placed with respect to the widening influence of modern Western industrial civilization. Mexico is but one of the peoples on that frontier of contact. Modern industrial civilization appears, offhand, to reach these marginal peoples as a sort of complex; those peoples that survive tend to react, it would seem, in ways different yet often comparable. Perhaps tractors, newspapers, linguistic revivals, technical manuals of craftsmanship, and a strong emotional attitude toward foreigners, compounded at once of admiration and contempt, represent recurrent elements in a describable process.

There is a growing disposition on the part of cultural anthropologists to study social processes as such, rather than to rest content with the mere description of cultures or the solution of specific historical sequences.

In large part ethnologists remain geographers and historians; they describe what is or was in that particular place, and tell how it got there. With many the scientific interest comes to rest in history, in the unraveling of another thread in the web of the past. Archaeologists and ethnologists together, by many detailed researches into the preliterary periods, have helped to make possible the "new history" of today.

Nevertheless the return to an interest in processual generalizations in the field of social anthropology, and the re-employment of what is essentially the comparative method, has in recent years been clearly marked. Anthropologists once more seek generalizations upon social change. With some, as with Wissler,[1] inquiries into the diffusion process have been made, not in order to sharpen tools for historical research, but in order to achieve control of contemporary and future change. Kroeber's more ultimate aim is at least in part that cultural anthropology shall cultivate "pure science,"[2] and the interest in culture process as distinct from culture history[3] is unequivocal in Malinowski.[4]

[1] *Man and Culture*, especially the chapter on "The Rationalization of the Culture Process"; also *The Relation of Nature to Man in Aboriginal America*.

[2] Address delivered before the Social Science Research Council, at Hanover, N.H., August 25, 1927, under the title "Study of Cultural Phenomena" (unpublished).

[3] The logic of this distinction is presented in A. L. Kroeber's "The Possibility of a Social Psychology." Radcliffe-Brown (art., "The Methods of Ethnology and Social Anthropology") makes the distinction quite clear, suggests a number of significant implications, and proposes the term "ethnology" for the historical discipline and "social anthropology" for the interest in arriving at natural laws of social change.

[4] "Whatever might be the value of an interest in origins of culture, it is obvious that unless these data bear in one way or another upon modern conditions,

If the interest of the student lies in an investigation of social processes in general terms, it would seem a more direct procedure to study such processes as they actually occur, rather than to content one's self with comparing the historical sequences so laboriously determined by historical methods of the ethnologist, who works without the direct sources of written records. In sequences of the latter sort only a small part of all the facts can ever be recaptured. If one is interested in studying what happens rather than what happened, one moves more directly if one studies it as it happens. Now that the power and personnel of anthropology has grown, it can undertake such investigations and still continue its work of preserving the record of the dying cultures.

That it is still possible to study the more isolated groups of Mexico in order to learn something about the pre-Columbian cultures, and about the changes

the purely antiquarian anthropology cannot be of great utility, and so far very little effort has been devoted to make evolutionary anthropology bear upon the actual problems of modern life.

"Again, the diffusionist writings, the reconstructions of past history of the various primitive races, is of no obvious or direct importance in modern questions. Whether mother-right has moved on the American continent from southeast to northwest, or whether moccasins were first discovered among the Algonquins of the northeast and gradually moved towards Mexico, this important historical fact has a theoretical significance perhaps, but it cannot very well be used by the social student in discussing prohibition, the negro problem, the question of divorce, of sexual morality, and so on.

"The recognition that social process is submitted to definite rules exactly as natural process is subject to the laws of physics, chemistry and biology, finds a very tenacious opposition in the science of society" (address under the title "Anthropology as a Social Science" before the Social Science Research Council at Hanover, N.H., August 10, 1926 [unpublished]).

which they underwent when they came in contact with
the Spaniards, is not to be denied. Such a study would
be a study of a dead culture and of a past change. It
is merely to be pointed out that such was not the interest which took the writer to Mexico. To learn as
much as can be learned as to the history of the present
culture of Tepoztlán is a part of any thorough study of
that culture. But the interest in the following pages
lies more particularly with the current changes. The
task was not conceived to be the rescue of survivals
from aboriginal culture. There was no attempt to collect, for example, folk songs persisting in the memory
of any individual which might most closely preserve
pre-Columbian characteristics, but rather to study
those songs which are today vivid and meaningful in
the lives of the contemporary folk. That these songs
are almost entirely European in character is interest-
ing, but in no way limits their importance.

The Mexican folk are not necessarily Indian. The
folk culture is a fusion of Indian and Spanish elements.
The acculturation which gave rise to this mixed culture took place three hundred years ago, largely within the first few generations after the Conquest. The
analysis of the Mexican folk culture into Spanish and
Indian elements is one problem—a historical problem.
The description of changes occurring in that folk culture due to spread of city ways is another problem—a
study of a contemporary change.

The disorganization and perhaps the reorganization

of the culture here considered under the slowly growing influence of the city is a process—a diffusion process—which can and will be studied. It is, the writer
assumes, an example, within convenient limits, of the
general type of change whereby primitive man becomes civilized man, the rustic becomes the urbanite.

CHAPTER I

THE VILLAGE OF TEPOZTLAN

The conspicuous fact in the social geography of Mexico is the dominance of the center over the margins. The great plateau in South-Central Mexico includes only one-sixth of the country but it contains two-thirds of the cities and nearly two-thirds of the population.[1]

The spider's solid body is held up in the center of a far-reaching circle of thin legs. Similarly the central plateau of Mexico, heavy with people, the center of population and government, looks out in all directions to thinly peopled corners of the country—empty Quintana Roo, scanty Chiapas, desert Sonora, and Lower California, unexplored western Sierras, dusty Chihuahua and Tamaulipas with its chaparral.[2]

Geographic factors in the first instance determine this distribution of population and of culture. The most favorable region in Mexico is that which is high enough to be healthful, where the rainfall is heavy enough to permit agriculture but not so heavy as to produce swamps, and where the relief is such as to allow the accumulation of level areas of fertile soil. This region is the central plateau; there the three geographic factors—altitude, rainfall, and relief—are conjointly favorable.

The Spanish-Indian civilization which occupies

[1] Sumner W. Cushing, art., "The Distribution of Population in Mexico."
[2] J. Russell Smith, *North America*, p. 777.

15

Mexico, like the Indian civilization which preceded it, depends on one subsistence crop—maize; and a map of the distribution of maize harvested in Mexico shows that production falls sharply away as one goes out from the central plateau.[1]

The plateau is the center of civilization, while the lowest cultures are found in isolated corners of the periphery. Mexico City, on the plateau, contains four times as many inhabitants as the second largest city (Guadalajara), and in it dwell a large majority of the professional men, scientists, and scholars of Mexico—most of those Mexicans who share in cosmopolitan culture. Those remnants of primitive peoples, on the other hand, that survive, are to be found in the extreme north where it is too dry, the extreme south where it is too wet, or in the isolated and precipitous western Sierra. The Tarahumare and the Tepehuane, the Cora and the Huichol, of the northwest, and the Lacandones and other tribes of the south, occupy the periphery, both geographical and cultural.

These aboriginal remnants and the sophisticated minority in the capital represent the two extremes of Mexican culture: the one urban in character and European in origin, and the other Indian and tribal. But the vast middle ground is occupied by people whose culture is neither tribal nor cosmopolitan. Their simple rural way of life is the product of ancient fusion between Indian and Spanish custom.

[1] C. C. Colby, *Source Book for the Economic Geography of North America*, p. 384.

This opposition between center and periphery exists also in political affairs. The plateau—the government in power—seeks always to protect itself against attacks directed inward against it from the margins of the country. Revolutions rarely have their origin on the plateau, but begin, as did the revolt of Díaz, in the south, or, as have most of the revolutions since, in the arid north.[1] The railways, and later the roads, reached out to connect the thinly settled parts of Mexico with the plateau.[2] Public security, along with thin population and low civilization, occupies a marginal position.

The central plateau is bounded on the north by a tableland which dips down northward into a region where the rainfall is too slight for agriculture. The aboriginal population here was sparse, and consisted chiefly of nomads. The settlements in this region are, therefore, nearly all post-Columbian. They are made possible by two changes which the Spaniards effected in the natural environment; the invaders found a use for the minerals there abundant and they introduced cattle.

On the other three sides the plateau is hemmed in by steep escarpments which rise three thousand feet above the plateau before falling sharply away to the sea. The eastern and western Sierras come together as the triangle which is Mexico north of the Isthmus

[1] Of course revolutions (except the Yaqui rebellions) originate among peoples of middle and upper culture, and are able to gain momentum because remote from the central power.

[2] Alexander Dye, art., "Railways and Revolutions in Mexico."

of Tehuantepec narrows toward the south, forming a
complex mountain system which largely occupies the
states of Michoacan, Morelos, Puebla, Guerrero, and
Oaxaca. The deep dissection of the highlands effected
by the Rio Papaloapam and the Rio de las Balsas
forms the third escarpment, having an east-west trend,
and bounding the plateau on the south.

The plateau and the three abutting escarpments
were the habitat of sedentary Indian tribes, of which
the Aztecs were the most conspicuous at the time of
the Conquest. The distribution of population in this
region, as contrasted with the north, has the same
character that it had in pre-Columbian days; and
many of the settlements continue in the new civilization a history and a *locus* which they already had in
the old.

The population of present-day Mexico, as was that
of aboriginal Mexico, is a village population. There
are almost no people living on scattered farms. Geography and history made this so. The generally arid and
mountainous nature of the country and the need for
common defense drew people together in close settlements. With this village tradition, developed among
agricultural tribes, the tradition of sixteenth-century
Spain was in accord. The Indian and the Castilian
pueblos were much alike; they blended easily into the
Mexican village of today.[1]

The villages are places out of which people go to
work and into which they go to trade. To fulfil their

[1] McBride, *Land Systems of Mexico.*

daily tasks, whether on their own *milpas*[1] on the margins of the town or in *haciendas*, mills, or mines still farther away, the male inhabitants scatter outside the village, returning at the end of the day, the week, or the season. But while the villagers live by agriculture, the village lives by trade. It is essentially a market, and the central *plaza*, where occur the periodic markets attended by people from other villages and where are situated all the public buildings and the private dwellings of size and importance, dominates and affords a focus for the town. The village, like Mexico itself, has a center and a periphery.

The state of Morelos lies upon the southern escarpment. It is the only state which lies entirely upon the slope; it forms one steep stairway up to the tableland. It is a small state, about the size of Delaware, but in its brief extent there is a descent of eight thousand feet. Its northern margin, the Sierra of Ajusco, which forms the southern rim of the great central basin, is a region of pine forests, chill winds, and charcoal-burners, while in the southern part of the state are tropical lowlands which produce coconuts and malaria.

Although only a small part of the state contains arable land,[2] nevertheless among the steep confusion of the mountains there are many sloping valleys which contain good soil and either receive sufficient rain or are watered by streams which arise in higher and wet-

[1] Small agricultural tracts cultivated by individuals for their own benefit.

[2] About 10 per cent, according to Francisco Bulnes, *The Whole Truth about Mexico*, p. 88.

ter regions. Therefore there are many villages, walled away one from another by the complicated mountains and lying one above the other on the steps of the stairway. Morelos is, indeed, one of the most densely populated states of Mexico.[1] But the population is one of small villages; there is no town with more than ten thousand inhabitants, and three-quarters of the people live in villages of less than two thousand.[2]

The state is entirely agricultural; there is practically no industry. Before the Conquest it was the seat of many Indian villages; these were united in loose economic and political federations, but each had its own patriotism and its own communal lands. The *hacienda* system, which had for its excuse in the north the geographic facts of an unpopulated region with few resources of water supply, lacked similar excuses in Morelos until the introduction of sugar cane. Sugar cane demands the construction of irrigation works and crushing machinery and so requires large-scale production. Because of this (and because of the early assignment of large groups of villages to individual conquerors as *encomiendas*), by 1910 the *hacienda* system had developed further in Morelos than anywhere else; indeed practically all the land belonged to the large estates of a few individuals.[3] Sugar made Morelos a

[1] In 1910, 84.7 inhabitants per square mile, and seventh in density of population among Mexican states, according to the computation from census figures of Wallace Thompson, *The People of Mexico*, p. 72.

[2] McBride, *Land Systems of Mexico*, p. 144.

[3] McBride says that only 140 of 28,000 heads of families were individual property-holders. One large *hacendado* owned seven times as much land as there was in all the small farms (under 1,000 *hectares*), in the state (*op. cit.*, pp. 143–44).

contributor to the wealth of Mexico, but it reduced the population to landless peonage. The revolution which began in 1910, especially in Morelos, may be regarded as the conflict between two social-economic systems: the one an ancient Indian tradition of self-sufficient and independent villages enjoying corporate land tenure, and the other a new capitalistic system of large-scale production of a money crop contributory to a world-economy. The agrarian reforms following the revolution broke up some of these estates. Others were kept together and operated by the state in an attempt to preserve the sugar plantations; but many lands where sugar was once grown have reverted to maize.

The northern border of Morelos lies along a part of the rampart which hems in the valley of Mexico. Going south from Mexico City, one climbs this valley wall, the Sierra of Ajusco, at an elevation of nine thousand feet above the sea. Standing upon the southern edge of the escarpment one stands also on the threshold of Morelos. There the rampart drops suddenly away into warm green valleys that go on and down one beyond the other in a maze of slighter mountains that from this eminence are no more than hills.

In each shelf or pocket of the mountains lies a village, or a cluster of villages. Close underneath the row of peaks[1] which forms the last bulwark of the escarpment is situated Tepoztlán. This village is the

[1] This *sierra*, the southwestern margin of the *cordillera* of Ajusco, extends southeastward to the *pueblo* of Tlayacapan, Morelos. It is composed of basaltic tufa and fine volcanic ash.

center of a cluster of villages which is not four miles in radius but which includes a descent of about twenty-five hundred feet, from San Juanico at an altitude of seven thousand feet to Santiago at about forty-five hundred.[1] These villages rest upon the topmost steps of the stairway, and these steps are the steepest.

Tepoztlán lies at the focus of a parabola of mountains the northern arm of which is the last escarpment wall. The southern arm is a range of somewhat lower mountains. The parabola opens southeastward; from Tepoztlán at its head the land slopes swiftly down to the valley of Yautepec. Thus Tepoztlán is not visible from the escarpment edge, but is hidden behind this screen of mountains, although from certain points almost half the extent of the state can be seen.

Whether the village is approached from above or from below it remains hidden in large part until it is actually entered. A density of trees, most of which bear either edible fruits or showy flowers, conceals the houses, which are all flat roofed and one story in height. Only the churches are taller; here and there they pierce the foliage. The great central church (*templo mayor*) on the *plaza* is by far the largest building in Tepoztlán; its great walls, crenelated to serve as battlements, and its two tall bell-towers dominate a village that, in the rainy season, escapes into and is lost in foliage.

[1] The *plaza* at Tepoztlán is at an altitude of about 1,700 meters (5,500 ft.) above sea-level.

Entering either from above or below one passes first through a belt of tilled ground: corn- and beanfields, each small plot separated from its neighbor by a wall made of heaped fragments of the abundant volcanic rubble. These are the *milpas;* by means of these little properties the villagers are fed, and to them their loyalties are bound.

The houses begin abruptly; they are set close beside the road; most are heavily shaded by trees. The streets are set with stones, rough hewn or placed just as they were found. Only near the *plaza* do the streets become wider, straighter, and smoother; those on the margins of the town are narrow and rough and often crooked. Most have steep grades; when this is so there is not a gradual gradient, but a series of alternating slants and levels. So the streets were laid out before the white men came. The method suggests the alternating stairways and platforms of the Indian *teocalli;* certainly it is adapted to a traffic made up solely of laden men and women; when the roads were first made there were no pack animals in Mexico. Today too the streets are very still; in them no wheel ever moves.

Tepoztlán was a *pueblo* of the Tlahuica, one of the Nahuatl-speaking tribes[1] that made up the last immigration south to the plateau region before the coming of the Spaniards. The ideograph of the town, an ax set in the sign for "mountain" or accompanied by

[1] Others were the Xochimilca, Chalca, Tepaneca, Acolhua, Tlaxcalteca, and Azteca.

the symbol meaning "place of,"[1] is found in several
of the ancient codices. The Codex Mendoza[2] lists Tepoztlán as one of the *pueblos* conquered by the Aztecs
under the elder Montezuma. The Codex Aubin-Gou-
pil[3] states that in 1487 new "kings" were installed in
Cuauhnahuac, Tepoztlán, Huaxtepec, and Xilotepec.
Cuauhnahuac was one of the first of the neighboring
pueblos to be conquered by the Aztecs; this town, and
presumably also Tepoztlán, became tributary to Tenochtitlan. The glyphs on the ruined *teocalli*,[4] situated
just above the town, contain the name of Ahuitzotl,
Aztec war chief, and a date which has been correlated
with modern chronology to read 1502 A.D.,[5] the last
year of his tenure of office.

Some one of the many gods generally shared by the
highland *pueblos* of Mexico was regarded as the special
protector of each one of the villages. That deity particularly associated with Tepoztlán was Ome Tochtli
("Two Rabbit"), the god generally described as that
of drunkenness,[6] but probably one also with genera-

[1] *Tepoztli* in Nahuatl meant "ax" and "copper"—and after the coming of the
Spaniards, also "iron." *Tlan* means "near," and is a common place-ending.
Rebus fashion, it is written by the picture of the incisor teeth (*tlantli*). Early
writings refer to the manufacture and trade in copper axes by the pre-Columbian
Tepoztecans.

[2] Plate IX of the Kingsborough reproduction.

[3] So says Edward Seler, art., "Die Tempelpyramide von Tepoztlan," p. 124.

[4] *Novello, Guia para visitar las principales ruinas arqueologicas del estado de
Morelos*, pp. 3–15.

[5] The year *Macuilli Tochtli* ("Ten Rabbit") (see Seler, *op. cit.*, p. 125).

[6] "This is an illustration of a grand debauch which a pueblo called Tepoztlán
celebrates as a ceremony. The custom was that when any Indian dies drunk, the
others of this pueblo held a grand ceremony, with axes of copper, which they use
for cutting wood in their hands. This pueblo is part of Yautepec, and its in-

tive attributes. The *teocalli* just referred to was presumably a temple of this god; his symbol appears on one of the glyphs. This temple is but one of a number of pre-Columbian structures which still exist on both sides of the present village of Tepoztlán. It was called to the attention of the scientific world by a native of the village, Ing. D. Francisco Rodriguez, in 1895, when it was cleared and studied.[1]

The god of the temple in his capacity as patron of Tepoztlán, or perhaps another closely associated with Ome Tochtli, was known as Tepoztecatl.[2] This name survives today in Tepoztlán as that of a legendary chieftain of the ancient *pueblo*. The ruined *teocalli* on the cliff above the town is known as the "house of Tepozteco." A number of tales, some of which are told not only locally but in other villages of South-Central Mexico, deal with the miraculous birth and heroic adventures of Tepoztecatl.[3] At a *fiesta* held once a year in Tepoztlán, a dance-drama commemorates the val-

---

habitants were vassals of the Marquis of the Valley" (commentary to p. 38 of the Codex Magliabecchi, trans. T. T. Waterman and published [1903] by the University of California Press as *The Book of Life of the Ancient Mexicans*).

[1] See Seler, *op. cit.*; Marshall H. Saville, art., "The Temple of Tepoztlán"; Francisco Rodriguez, art., "Descripción de la piramide llamada Casa del Tepozteco"; Manuel Miranda y Marron, art., "Una excursión a Tepoztlán, Morelos. El teocalli de Ometochtli."

[2] His representation appears on p. 23 of the manuscript in the National Library of Florence. The face, of two colors, bears a semilunar nose ornament (*yacameztli*); the figure carries a shield and a hatchet. Early references to Tepoztecatl are collected by González Casanova, in art., "El ciclo legendario del Tepoztecatl," pp. 18–25.

[3] Three stories of this character, two from Tepoztlán and one from Milpa Alta, Distrito Federal, are published i n Nahuatl text and Spanish translation by P. González Casanova, *op. cit.*

orous defense of Tepoztlán by Tepoztecatl against the attacks of neighboring *pueblos*. These tales and this ritual are but dim echoes of ancient memories, although they constitute an important part of the more ancient lore; they lie upon the margins of attention in the Tepoztlán of today.

A document apparently written in 1580[1] gives some information as to Tepoztlán before and just after the Conquest. The inhabitants sold in neighboring *pueblos* the wood that abounded on their hillsides and the lime to be found in their territory. Their principal industry was the making of paper of fiber obtained from a tree. The name of this commodity (*amatl*) survives today in the name of one of the villages in the valley (Amatlan), and the grooved-stone pulp-beaters used in the ancient industry are among the commonest of pre-Columbian artifacts to be encountered in the valley.

The Spaniard first entered Tepoztlán in 1521. In that year, the same which saw the subjugation of Tenochtitlan, Cortés passed through Tepoztlán on his way to Cuernavaca from Yautepec. "There we found many pretty women and much loot," says Bernal Díaz del Castillo. As certain Yautepec chieftains there seeking refuge would not give themselves up, the Spaniards set fire to half the town.[2] Later, Tepoztlán

---

[1] The "Relación de Tepoztlán," published by Francisco Plancarte in the *Boletin oficial y revista eclesiastica del obispade de Cuernavaca*, X, 313–17, 326–31, and 348–52, and cited in Miguel Salinas, art., "La Sierra de Tepoztlán," pp. 362 ff.

[2] Bernal Díaz del Castillo, *The Conquest of New Spain*, Book X, chap. cxliv (IV, 67, of the Hakluyt translation).

was one of the *pueblos* awarded to Cortés as *en-comienda*.[1] After his death the village was reputedly the residence of his son, Martin Cortés; and fragments of heavy wall opposite the chapel of La Santísima are pointed out as vestiges of his house.

Tepoztlán was not the seat of resident Catholic missionaries in the first years following the Conquest.[2] The priests of Yautepec and Oaxtepec, too busy in these *pueblos* to give spiritual attention to Tepoztlán, asked the viceroy[3] to send missionaries to Tepoztlán; and some time during the third quarter of the sixteenth century this was done. The region which now forms the state of Morelos was divided into three zones, running from north to south: the western zone was intrusted to the Franciscans, the eastern to the Augustinians, and the central zone to the Dominicans. Tepoztlán fell within the central zone. The Dominicans at once began the conversion of the natives and the construction of the great church and accompanying monastery, which still stand today, little changed.[4]

The conversion of the Tepoztecos was intrusted to Fr. Domingo de la Anunciación. He was a Dominican priest of more than ordinary repute; he had taken part

[1] *Colección de documentos inéditos del Real Archivo de Indias*, XII, 554–63.

[2] A historical sketch of Tepoztlán is included by Miguel Salinas in *op. cit.* His account is based on the "Relación de Tepoztlán," just cited, on an old document then in the possession of José G. González, native and priest of Tepoztlán—two sources not directly available to the present writer—and on information supplied Salinas by residents of the *pueblo*. The historical data included in the rest of this chapter are drawn from Salinas' account.

[3] Luis de Velasco, who held office from 1550 to 1564.

[4] The González document states that the church was completed in 1588.

in one of the Spanish expeditions to Florida. Fr. Domingo undertook at once the overthrow of the patron
god of the *pueblo*, Ome Tochtli, or Tepoztecatl, a
deity of such importance that pilgrims came from as
far as Chiapas to visit his altar. Tradition has it that
he persuaded the Indians to allow him to put the
power of Ome Tochtli to a test. He would hurl the
figure from its eminence on the cliff above the valley;
if it should be dashed into pieces the natives would
acknowledge its lack of divine power. The test was
carried out; the idol smashed into fragments on the
rocks; these fragments were incorporated into the
foundations of the Christian church. The stone cross
under the *ahuehuetes* around the well-watered clearing
at the place known as Axihtla, at the northern edge of
the *pueblo*, is supposed to mark the spot where the
first baptisms took place.

During the early part of the colonial period the
forms of Christianity and the few important elements
of Spanish material culture—iron, plow, cattle, swine,
and fruit trees—became incorporated into an Indian
culture that had been stripped by the *padres* of most
traits of primitive ritual and belief. The *pueblo* pros-
pered; the streets were improved, new aqueducts built,
a walled garden with a bandstand erected in the central square. The first municipal government was installed in 1820. During the nineteenth century periods of prosperity alternated with periods of decline.
The old documents report pestilences in 1813, 1814,
1830, and 1833. In 1839 an earthquake shook down

the towers of the church. Periods of revolution temporarily scattered the people and retarded development.

In the second half of the nineteenth century Tepoztlán reached its highest level of development. This was largely due to the activities of José Guadalupe Rojas, and later members of the same family. Under their influence the schools of the church were supplemented by night schools for adults, an attempt was made to publish a local newspaper; an "academy" was founded for the conduct of discussions in the Nahuatl language. This period of local brilliance coincided with the general peace attending the régime of Díaz. Much of the sophistication attained during this era was lost during the revolution of 1910–21. Then for a time Tepoztlán was entirely depopulated, and intellectuals, such as the members of the Rojas family, never returned.

After the first invasion of conqueror and of priest, it is doubtful if many persons of Spanish blood came to live in Tepoztlán.[1] The contacts with Europeans were effected by the movement of Tepoztecans to Mexico City or to other cities. These movements, frequent and accelerated by periods of revolution, have continued for four centuries. In a straight line—if it

[1] A document in the National Library of Paris, dating from the last decade of the seventeenth century or the first decade of the eighteenth, includes a census of *pueblos* in the Cuernavaca region. This gives for Tepoztlán 885 heads of families (*vecinos*), 2,628 persons (*almas*), that were Indians; 55 heads of families, 223 persons of *otras castas*—no doubt whites and *mestizos* (Manuel Mazari, art., "Un antiguo padrón itinerario del estado de Morelos," p. 151). The amount of white blood probably declined after this period.

is profitable to speak of straight lines in a country
where no communication is straight—Mexico City is
no more than fifty miles from Tepoztlán. Yet, in spite
of this, and in spite of the testimony of Bernal Díaz,
the Tepoztecans today appear to be Indians of almost
pure blood. Out of four thousand native inhabitants
not more than a score or two show plainly their white
blood. The Nahuatl language persists, and is spoken
by nearly all the inhabitants.[1] A number of young
people speak it only as a second language of much
less familiarity. On the other hand, nearly everyone
speaks Spanish; there are a few old people who do not,
and many to whom Spanish is the less familiar tongue.
The essential bilinguality of the population reflects
the even balance of the culture between Indian and
European elements; the culture is neither aboriginal
nor Spanish, but a close integration of both—it is
Mexican. The inhabitant of Mexico, generally speaking, is the product of these two heritages. But in Tepoztlán, a *pueblo* which was long established before
the Conquest on the site which it still occupies and
which began immediately after the Conquest to receive elements of European culture, the community
itself is the product of that fusion.

[1] The Nahuatl spoken in Tepoztlán, and especially differences in phonetic
pattern between Tepoztecan Nahuatl and "classical" Nahuatl, are treated by
González Casanova in *Un cuento Mexicano*.

CHAPTER II
THE MATERIAL CULTURE

The material culture of Tepoztlán, in contrast to the non-material culture, preserves unmodified a large number of pre-Columbian traits.[1] The small number of the conquerors brought with them no great economic system with which to displace that already in operation among the Indians. The Mexican village did not, even before the Conquest, make all its own tools; villages specialized then, as now, in the manufacture of a few useful articles and imported the rest from other manufacturing centers.

With the exception of ironworking, which soon made obsolete the Indian techniques in stone, bone, shell, and copper, most of the elements contributed to the material culture by the Spaniards supplement rather than supplant technical systems of the Indians. Pre-Columbian patterns persist especially in the house, in house furnishings, and in cookery. Here there are many contributions from European culture, but these remain of secondary importance. The old techniques survive also in transportation, but there the post-

[1] Bandelier gave us a short account (A. F. Bandelier, *Report of an Archaeological Tour in Mexico in 1881*, "Papers of the Archaeological Institute of America, American Series" [Boston, 1884], II, 95–99, 120–52) of the material culture of Cholula in the state of Puebla, and Starr (Frederick Starr, *Notes upon the Ethnography of Southern Mexico*, reprinted from Vols. VIII and IX, *Proceedings of Davenport Academy of Natural Sciences*, Davenport, Iowa, 1900) has scattered notes on the material culture of many villages in Southern Mexico.

Columbian contributions are of much greater relative importance. Finally, clothing, especially that of women, is an aspect of material culture where Indian elements have been almost entirely supplanted by European.

The house group is the dwelling of a single family with accompanying outbuildings. As house sites are almost always walled off from the streets and as houses are rebuilt upon the rubble of earlier structures, the house, except near the central *plaza*, is usually above the level of the street. The house is always rectangular. The walls are most commonly of *adobe*; but may be of rough stones set in a mud mortar, or withes, wattle, or cornstalk. The roof, except where poverty prescribes mere thatching, is of tiles (a European improvement); the roofs are almost flat. There is ordinarily only one entrance to a room. Where there is more than one room, passage from one to another may most commonly be effected only by going outside and entering the single entrance of the adjoining room. Window openings, except in the more Europeanized houses near the *plaza*, are rare. Glass windows and screening are practically unknown. Floors are of dirt.

Where wealth or Spanish influence has been stronger, most particularly in buildings near the central *plaza*, the form of the house may be modified in one or more of the following respects: The rooms are grouped around a *patio*. A roofed corridor runs around the inside of this. Or, much more commonly, the single room is fronted by a roofed porch, built integral with the house. The roof of this porch is supported by columns; there may be an arch or two. The roof may be peaked. The porch (*corredor*), and perhaps also the house, has a brick floor. There are several windows; some of these contain iron grilles. The walls are plastered and perhaps tinted.

However mean or however important, the house is ornamented by a number of flowering plants, usually potted in oilcans, and stood outside the house on a rack.

The tripartite house division into *sala*, kitchen and storehouse, emphasized by Bandelier[1] and well illustrated by Starr,[2] is not always clearly marked. Sometimes the kitchen is merely a flimsy lean-to against the house, or is in a corner of the *corredor*, or is even in a corner of the single room. But more often it is a separate room or even an entirely separate structure.

The storehouse (S. *troje*)[3] is practically always present, and is usually placed immediately in front of the dwelling. It occurs in three forms, all of which are probably of entirely pre-Columbian design. The *ohuatlapil* (N. *ohuatlapilli*) is most common. This is circular, about six feet high and of varying diameter; it is made of vertical cornstalks bound together with rope. It contains maize on the cob (S. *mazorca*). Also made to contain *mazorca* is the *cincolote* (N. *zincolohtli*). This is square, of poles laid horizontally, one pair upon

[1] *Op. cit.*, p. 129.

[2] Frederick Starr, *Indians of Southern Mexico, An Ethnographic Album* (Chicago, 1899), Plates XLIV, XLV, XLVI, XLVII.

[3] "S." indicates term used in Spanish discourse; "N.," term used in Nahuatl discourse.

another at right angles to the first until a structure is raised tall enough to contain the maize to be stored. The *cuezcomate* (N. *cuezcomatl*) is a vasiform granary, plastered inside and out with clay. In it is kept shelled corn.

Perhaps every fourth dwelling has a sweathouse (S. *temazcal;* N. *temazcalli*), well known as a part of the pre-Columbian house group. This is made of stone set in mortar. It is rectangular, approximately square, and about five feet high at the center. The roof is low peaked. The one entrance is barely large enough to permit entrance of a man on hands and knees. Although occasionally now used merely to achieve cleanliness, its use, as in pre-Columbian times, is chiefly therapeutic.

These are all indigenous features. Although bees and turkeys were domesticated before the Conquest, it is not clear to what extent the beehive—a simple wooden box—and the fowlhouse preserve pre-Columbian elements. The fowlhouse (S. *gallinero;* N. *pizcalli*) is a part of nearly every domestic establishment (but in many homes some of the chickens perch on ladders in a corner of the dwelling). It is usually built of stone, to keep out marauding carnivores, and has about the size and form of the sweathouse, except that the roof is tiled. To protect a horse or *burro* a thatched or tiled roof is erected in a corner of the yard. Something in which to store water completes the house group. This is either a plastered tank (S. *pila*) or a large jar (S. *tianja;* N. *acomitl*) or merely an alcohol tin.

Neglecting for a moment the additional furnishings of the more urbanized and well to do, one may declare the domestic equipment within the house to be almost entirely pre-Columbian. The kitchen is the center of domestic activity, and around it cluster most of the accessories. Four features are inevitably present in all houses, of whatever poverty or pretensions. These four features vary hardly at all in form or position,[1] and preserve, hardly modified at all, pre-Columbian form and function. These four are the hearth, the griddle, the grinding-stone, and the pot. The hearth (S. *tlequil;* N. *tlequilitl*) is sometimes no more than three stones set in a triangle to support the griddle; but more often it is of many stones, plastered, and horseshoe shaped. Upon it fits the griddle (S. *comal;* N. *comalli*), a flat, circular tray, which occurs in only one diameter (about eighteen inches). Although griddles of iron are common in the cities, in Tepoztlán they are always of clay. When not in use the griddle stands on edge at the back of the *tlequil.* The three-legged grinding-stones (S. *metate;* N. *metlatl*) with their long handstone (S. *metlapil;* N. *metlapilli*) are of the well-known pattern. They are of andesite. The pot in which the maize is cooked (S. *olla de nixtamal;* N. *nexcomitl*) stands beside the hearth.

In some houses the *tlequil,* which burns wood, is supplemented by the brazier (S. *brasero*) of Spanish origin. This burns charcoal. It may be of iron and brought from the city, or it may be a homemade copy

[1] Cf. Bandelier, *op. cit.,* p. 138; Starr, *Notes on the Ethnography* . . . . , p. 3.

in stone and clay. Only a small part of cookery in Tepoztlán is done on the brazier.

Most of the other articles which contribute to culinary technique are Indian, not European. The small andesite mortar (S. *molcajete;* N. *molcaxitl*) and the pestle (S. *tejolote;* N. *texolotl*) are used chiefly for grinding *chile*. Two of the three common forms of basket are likewise pre-Columbian in general character. These are the forms without handles: the *chiquihuite* (N. *xiquihuitl*), which is stiff, as wide as it is deep, and coiled on splints; and the *tompiate* (N. *tompiatl*), which is flexible, twice as deep as it is wide, and woven of soft reed. The other basket, which is of the shape of an ordinary European market basket, with a handle, has no Nahuatl name (it is always called *canasta*), and is apparently a form introduced by the Spaniards. Its principal use is in marketing; therefore it is carried only by women, and on the left arm under the *rebozo*. The whole forms a *canasta-rebozo* minor complex of post-Columbian development. The other two baskets are used for the storage and transport of food (the *chiquihuite* is also used to strain honey), and may be carried by either man or woman.

Mexican pottery has been much modified since the Conquest. Many forms are European, and the ware is in general inferior. Shell-decorated Cuernavaca pottery is common in Tepoztlán, and there are occasional pieces of glazed and painted Oaxaca ware. The ware in general use in cookery is the plain ware of Toluca. The pot (S. *olla;* N. *xoctli*) preserves the ancient form;

the pitcher (S. *jarro*) and the saucer (S. *cazuela*) are more European than Indian and are mentioned by the Spanish names only.

Minor elements in the culinary paraphernalia are the shallow wooden boat-shaped mixing bowl (S. *batea*), the wooden spoon (S. *batedor*), and the small, rectangular, handled fan (S. *aventador*) with which the fire is blown up. For picking fruit from trees a cage-like picker of cane, on the end of a long pole, is employed. This is called (S.) *canastilla* or (N.) *acatecomatl*.

Other house furnishings vary considerably with the wealth and education of the owner. Characteristically, however, the bed (S. *cama;* N. *tlapechtli*) is a mat (S. *petate;* N. *petlatl*) spread on the ground or on a low wooden platform. Often another aboriginal form of bed is used: splints of Mexican *bambú* (S. *otate;* N. *ohtlatl*) are stretched in both directions across a framework of low posts driven in the ground. Tables are common but often absent in poorer houses. The backed chair is not rare, but much commoner is the low, backless bench. Although occasionally reminiscent of the pre-Columbian *icpalli*, it nevertheless is generally European in form. No adult sleeps in a hammock, but babies are usually cradled in a flat, swinging framework which is homemade. This resembles other Indian cradle-frames, but bears the Taino name *hamaca*.

Certain domestic accessories of European origin have become firmly associated with the aboriginal elements and are always found in the house. Chief among these are the steel knife, the small iron kerosene flare

(S. *candil*), the candle, and the alcohol tin (S. *bote*) in which water is carried and stored. Two of these tins are yoked together and swung over the shoulder. In this device (S. *aguantador*), of course European in character, water is hauled by the men. A woman carries only a single tin.

A domestic shrine is found in most houses. This may be no more than a printed or painted picture of a saint, but more commonly it is a carved and painted wooden figure, usually a Virgin or a Christ. This may be only a few inches high, or as much as six feet. Most are from early Colonial times. In front of this figure an incense burner (S. *sahumeria;* N. *popochcomitl*) is placed. This is of black glazed pottery. In it copal gum is burned. Flowers are also placed before the figure, in bottles or vases, and pictures of other saints are hung near the image. This shrine is the center of domestic worship and ritual. Candles are burned before it on feast days; here the infant Christ is "put to bed" on Christmas Eve and taken up on Candlemas; before this image are placed gifts brought on birthdays or those brought by a boy's parents during the negotiations leading to a marriage with a daughter of the house.

Any property not in use is kept on plain wooden shelves or in covered wooden chests. Extra clothing is hung on nails. Walls are frequently decorated with pictures cut from newspapers, with sentimental picture postcards, and with little clay toys and ornamental dishes brought from other villages.

This description of the domestic equipment relates to most of the houses in Tepoztlán. A conspicuous minority, however, as has already been indicated, enjoy elements of modern industrial civilization. A house of this limited class may possess a few china dishes, or a few glasses, some metal pans, perhaps a sideboard or a metal bed or even a phonograph. The sewing machine alone, however, among modern machines, has become a part of the general Tepoztecan material culture; it is found in all parts of the village and in houses otherwise Indian in character.

Cookery[1] has been but slightly modified by European elements. The most important foodstuffs contributed by European culture are beef, pork, sugar, rice, chickens, eggs, and milk. Less important contributions are potatoes, lima beans, wheat flour, chickpeas, citrus fruits, and spices. The maize-squash-beans complex remains, however, the basis of cookery. These staples were and still are cooked with *chiles* and tomatoes. Honey is still used as a sweetening, but has been largely supplanted by cane sugar. Cinnamon has displaced the native vanilla. The apparatus of cookery and the accompanying techniques are almost untouched by European influence. Maize is boiled with lime and ground on the *metate* to a dough which is the basis of a variety of foods. Chief among these is the *tortilla* (N. *tlaxcalli*), the inevitable griddle-bread which accompanies every meal both as a food and as an eat-

[1] See Margaret Park Redfield, art., "Notes on the Cookery of Tepoztlán, Morelos."

ing utensil. The principal variations on the *tortilla* are forms to which shortening has been added (S. *itacates;* N. *itacatl;* S. *clacloyos;* N. *tlatoyos;* S. *gorditas*), and *tortillas* filled with *chiles*, beans, or other foods (S. *memelitas*, N. *tlaxcalmimilli;* S. *tacos;* S. *migajes*, N. *xalli*). These variations are devised to carry food away from the house or to keep it edible some time after preparation. The same dough, stirred in water and strained, forms the basis of gruels (S. *atoles;* N. *atolli*), which are flavored in several different ways. These were a daily food in pre-Columbian times, but in Tepoztlán today they do not constitute a regular part of the daily fare.[1] To the same dough fat is added, and sometimes other ingredients, to prepare *tamales* (N. *tamalli*), which are rolls of this dough boiled in corn husks. Although the sweetened *tamal* is prepared to sell at the nearest railway station, in Tepoztlán itself the *tamal* is never a part of the daily fare; but, as in ancient days, is eaten only at *fiestas*.

Another pre-Columbian food category of undiminished importance includes the *moles* (N. *molli*). These are highly spiced sauces served with pieces of boiled meat. The spices are ground in the *molcajete* or on the *metate*. There are three *moles*, two festal and one secular. The last is a relatively simple sauce, chiefly of *chile*, served with pork or beef. It is often eaten at breakfast. *Mole verde* is a more complex combination of elements, served usually with beef. It is never served without *tamales*, and only at *fiestas* celebrating

[1] As they do, for example, in Cholula (Bandelier, *op. cit.*, p. 138).

a *santo*. *Mole poblano* (or "turkey *mole*" [S. *mole de guajolote;* N. *huexolomolli*]) in Tepoztlán may be made of as many as nineteen ingredients. It is always served with turkey and only on the occasion of very important *fiestas*, characteristically weddings and baptisms.

Another category, *tortas*, includes vegetables, potatoes, etc., which are ground, mixed with egg, fried, and served with *chile*. These represent an application of the aboriginal grinding- and *chile*-patterns to introduced foods.

The cultivated and purchased foods are supplemented with a number of wild vegetable foods and occasionally game.

It will be observed that a very few techniques of cookery are employed. Foods are boiled, fried, or toasted. In spite of the presence of the oven, used by bakers and pastry-makers, domestic food is never roasted or baked.

Three meals a day are generally eaten. *Tortillas* and beans are found at nearly every meal; often there is little or nothing else. Meat is most frequently added.

The commonest beverage is coffee, home grown and toasted. Chocolate, the aboriginal drink, is everywhere known but its use is restricted by its cost. When made, it is beaten to a froth in the ancient manner. Milk is not rarely drunk, but usually sweetened with sugar or flavored with chocolate; it is almost never used as an ingredient in cookery. A variety of "teas" are made of native and also of introduced herbs and seeds. Commercial sugar-cane alcohol is largely drunk by the men. The maguey does not flourish at this low altitude; therefore *pulque* (anciently *octli*) must be imported, and its use is confined largely to festal occasions.

The ancient male costume of the Aztecs, although modified according to the social position of the wearer, was composed of three principal garments: the *maxtlatl*, a belt or loincloth with the ends hanging down in front like an apron; the *tilmahtli*, a woven cape worn over the shoulders and knotted in front; and the *cactli*, sandals of leather or woven of maguey fiber. Of these three the first has entirely disappeared,[1] the second influenced the form and use of the modern *zarape*, while the third remains little changed today. For all articles of men's clothing worn today in Tepoztlán, Nahuatl terms are in use. The ancient term *tilmahtl* is applied to the *zarape*, and the sandals are still called *cactli* or *cuitlax-cactli* ("leather sandals"). The other terms are descriptive compositions, or are Spanish roots modified to suit Nahuatl linguistic patterns.

A man wears one or more shirts (S. *camisa;* N. *cotontli*) and over these, when the weather is colder or for better dress, a blouse (S. *blusa;* N. *panicotontli*). These, like the trousers, are made of cheap white cotton cloth bought in the local stores and are made up by the women. The blouse is buttonless; the lower ends tie together in front. For holiday attire the shirt may be pink or blue, or a colored vest (S. *chaleco*)

[1] It may possibly be worn by some in Tepoztlán, as it still is elsewhere in Mexico (*ibid.*, p. 121).

may be added. Loose white trousers (S. *calzones;* N. *cahzon*) of the same material are worn. These are wide at the waist; the sides are crossed in front and the trousers are held up by a cloth belt or sash (S. *faja* or *ceñidor;* N. *teilpiloni*). A man often goes barefoot. The sandals are of the ancient pattern except that steer leather is used. A woman does not wear sandals except when traveling. The straw hat (S. *sombrero;* N. *cuatlayecahuilotl*), worn almost everywhere in Mexico, is of course of Spanish origin. A few styles are "correct" in Tepoztlán.

It remains to mention the *zarape*. Ramon Mena[1] derives the word from Nahuatl *tzalanpepechtli* (*tzalan*, "interwoven," and *pepechtli*, "thick blanket"), a descriptive term applied by the Indians to the heavy blankets, often woven in with metal threads, carried by the conquerors and placed by them upon the ground when resting or sleeping. This blanket and the *tilmahtli* fused, culturally, and became the *zarape*. In Tepoztlán two forms are worn: the blanket form, wrapped around the shoulders and held together with one arm, and the *poncho* form,[2] in which the head passes through an opening in the center. The *zarape* is entirely masculine, but on unusually cold days a woman may borrow a *zarape* and wear it beneath her *rebozo*.

The *machete* (N. *tlateconi* or *tepoztlateconi*), the characteristic Mexican steel knife with the curved tip, is

[1] Ramon Mena, "El Zarape," *Anales del Museo Nacional de Arqeologia, Historia y Etnografia* (época 5ª), I, No. 4 (Sept.–Oct., 1925), 373 ff.

[2] This *poncho* is probably South American in origin.

so generally carried that it may be mentioned as a part of the costume.

The woman's costume in Tepoztlán preserves fewer indigenous elements, although this is not the case in many other villages in Southern Mexico. Before the Conquest it consisted of two principal garments: a loose blouse (*huipilli*) and a skirt (*cueitl*), consisting of a rectangular cloth wrapped around the lower part of the body. The *huipilli*, under that same name, is worn in many Indian communities south of Morelos, but not in Tepoztlán. In Tepoztlán the woman's costume is European in origin, and the names of the garments in Nahuatl discourse are Spanish, except those for the skirts, which are descriptive Nahuatl terms.

Over white cotton underdrawers (S. *pantelones;* N. *pantelontin*) is worn an underskirt (S. *enaguas adentro;* N. *cueiztactli*), usually also white, and over this a colored overskirt (S. *enaguas encima;* N. *cueipanitl*). The skirts are ankle length, very full, and gored. A collarless shirt (S. *camisa;* N. *camisahtin*), tucked into the skirt, covers the upper part of the body. Over it is worn a blouse (S. *saco;* N. *sacohtin*), and over this usually an apron. This either includes an upper piece covering the chest, when it is called (S.) *babero,* (N.) *baberohtin,* or does not, when it is called (S.) *delantal,* (N.) *delantaltin.* Around the waist is wound a sash (S. *ceñidor;* N. *zinidor*), dark blue or gray, about eight inches wide and six to ten feet long. This is the only garment of those here enumerated which is woven in

Tepoztlán. Almost invariably there are earrings, often of gold (S. *aretes;* N. *areteztin*), and a short string of beads, most commonly red seeds (N. *corales;* N. *coraleztin*). Except when walking long distances, when sandals may be worn, or when in city dress, which includes shoes, the feet are bare. The only overgarment is the *rebozo* (N. *payo*), a sort of shawl worn over the head and upper body; one end is drawn across the breast and thrown back over the left shoulder. This is the characteristically Mexican garment worn almost everywhere and by every class except the highest. The *rebozo*, like the *zarape*, is a post-Conquest development, but unlike the *zarape* it has no Indian progenitor. It probably represents a cheaper and more practical modification of the Spanish *mantilla* by the working Indian woman; and it had already taken its form by the end of the sixteenth century.[1]

Many women possess, for Sunday costume, a one-piece dress of finer material. This is nearly always white, with a flounced skirt, and ornamented with pink or blue ribbons.

No woman ever wears a hat except when a man's hat is worn for work in the fields or traveling in the sun. When sitting in the sun a woman may wind the *rebozo* on her head like a turban, but the real turban headdress frequently found in Southern Mexico is absent. The hair is worn in two braids, or, particularly by girls and young women, in a single braid. No cos-

[1] José de J. Nuñez y Dominguez, *El rebozo*. Mexico: Departamento Editorial de la Dirección General de las Bellas Artes, 1917.

metics are used except that at the carnival talcum powder may be put on the face.

Two generations ago the prevailing woman's costume in Tepoztlán was of another sort, a sort which included more aboriginal elements. This costume still survives in Tepoztlán, where two or three old women still wear it; there are probably others in the neighboring hamlets. It consisted of two principal garments: a skirt (N. *pitzcueitl*), of homespun, white above the hip and black below, where it was pleated; and a white triangle of similar homespun worn over the head like a *poncho* with one corner hanging down the back. This latter garment is the *quechquemitl*. It is a probably indigenous garment worn by Indian women in Central and Northern Mexico.

These two garments were made locally on primitive looms. Today all textiles are imported either as ready-made garments or as cloth to make up into clothing, except some of the women's belts which are still made locally.

The children's clothing reproduces that of the adults.

The aboriginal transportation system and that introduced by the Spaniards exist side by side in Tepoztlán, as they do nearly everywhere in Mexico. *Burros*, mules, horses, and oxen, with the accompanying paraphernalia—saddles, bridles, lassos, yokes—are used in patterns substantially those of sixteenth-century Spain. Only the wheel is not used in Tepoztlán, because the steepness and rockiness of the roads make its use impossible.

Nevertheless a very large part of transport takes place on human backs with the aid of aboriginal devices. Burdens are supported with the aid of the forehead tump-line (S. *mecapal;* N. *mecapalli*), which is sometimes assisted by another line across the chest. Articles are carried either in the *chiquihuite*, which is then bound to the *mecapal* by means of the *ayate* (N. *ayatl*),[1] a tough, coarse-woven cloth of maguey fiber, or else in the *huacal* (N. *huacalli*), a crate of rough-hewn sticks. Water is carried in a hollow gourd (S. *bule;* N. *atecomatl*), supported by a lacing of leather thongs. Women, as has already been said, carry purchases or small belongings in the *canasta*, or occasionally in a long rectangular fiber bag (S. *bolsa*). Men never carry these, but use for the *machete* or other possessions a small flat, square bag of vegetable fiber, the *morral* (S.).

Of musical instruments, recognized by the Tepoztecans as such, all are European: guitar, flute, saxophone, cornet, etc. Ritual music is sharply distinguished and ordinarily not called music. Of instruments employed for this purpose the horizontal wooden double-slotted drum (*teponaztli*) is entirely pre-Columbian. One of the two *teponaztlis* remaining in Tepoztlán has every appearance of being an actual pre-Columbian artifact. The *huehuetl*, the vertical drum with the skin head, which in Mexico is a commoner survival than the *teponaztli*, does not occur in

[1] On the use of the *ayate* among the Otomi see Starr, *Notes on the Ethnography of Southern Mexico*, p. 8.

Tepoztlán. The small flageolet (S. *chirimía*), which together with a small drum of European pattern is played on the roof of the church or chapel to signalize every sacred *fiesta*, as were once played on the *teocalli* the *tlapitsali*, *huehuetl*, and *teponaztli*, is carved out of *zopilote* wood and is a modification of the ancient pattern under Spanish influence. In Nahuatl discourse it bears the ancient name *tlapitsali*.

Local industries are few and almost all are European in character. *Adobe* bricks are made by anyone who builds a new house or repairs an old one; the simple technique is probably chiefly aboriginal. The twisting of ropes of maguey fiber is a domestic industry confined to a limited group of houses. This technique is European; a wooden wheel is used. The lime-burning done at the neighboring hamlet of San Andres is likewise European. Carpentering, ironworking, masonry, woodcarving, silverwork, shoemaking, and breadmaking are all in the hands of specialists; in each case the tools and techniques are European—the early priests were good teachers and the Indians good pupils.

Mena[1] declares that *zarapes* are made in Tepoztlán of tree cotton, but other evidence of such manufacture is lacking. A large loom has recently been introduced by an educated young man for the weaving of shawls. The use of tree cotton (N. *cuahichcatl*) is, however, well understood, and occasionally thread is spun thereof by the use of pre-Columbian spindle

[1] *Op. cit.*, p. 382.

whorls (S. *malacate;* N. *malacatl*) which abound in
Tepoztlán and are simply picked up in any yard and
used. Even in the few surviving primitive looms, however, commercial thread is used. There are at least
two of these looms still in operation in Tepoztlán.
They are used only to weave women's belts. The
structure and somewhat detailed nomenclature of this
loom cannot find room for discussion here. The weft
is set up on a framework (N. *tzatzaztin*) of ten short
sticks driven into the ground. The upper end of the
loom is fastened to a house or tree; the lower end is
drawn tight with the backstrap (N. *analoni*).[1]

Of industries relying on special machinery there are
two: the mill, to which is brought for grinding only a
small part of the maize eaten in Tepoztlán,[2] and the
mixing and bottling of soft drinks of carbonated water
and artificial flavoring. Several men are occupied with
this enterprise, and the product is largely consumed.

This fusion of Indian with Spanish features produces, it will readily be seen, three classes of culture
traits: unaltered Indian elements; elements which
have developed in Mexico from the impinging of
Spanish features upon a homologous Indian pattern;
and European elements transported intact to Mexico.

---

[1] Mena says, and probably rightly, that the entire loom is called *analoni*.
But these particular informants used the term for the backstrap only.

[2] There are three reasons why the mill has only a limited use: to many the
slight cost is prohibitive; husbands assert that the flavor of *tortillas* made of
mill-ground *nixtamal* is very inferior; and, finally, to bring her maize regularly
to the mill to the neglect of her *metate* lowers a woman in her neighbors' eyes.

These three classes are respectively represented, for example, in costume by the sandals, the *zarape*, and the trousers, and in agricultural tools by the pointed stick, the *coa*,[1] and the plow. But while a separation of Indian from European elements is of interest to the culture-historian, it is of no interest to the native of Tepoztlán. The integration of certain European elements with Indian features is complete. Although few introduced elements bear completely Nahuatl names (the *machete* is one exception),[2] the Tepoztecan is unconscious of any difference between these and pre-Columbian elements. He feels the same with regard to his sandals, which are almost wholly Indian in origin, as he does with regard to his white trousers, which are wholly European. The *machete* is as Mexican as the *petate*.

There is, however, a grouping of culture traits which corresponds to the prevailing attitude of the Tepoztecans themselves. So far as surviving Indian elements and as certain European elements are concerned, the integration is complete. The culture just described, involving elements of both cultural heritages, is that which is general throughout Tepoztlán. But not all of

---

[1] The *coa* is the flat iron hoe with the blade set parallel with the handle. It preserves the curved edge and the function (it is used to heap up earth around the maize) of the aboriginal *huictli*, but it is now made of iron and has probably somewhat changed its shape.

[2] In speaking Nahuatl one uses the Spanish word modified to fit Nahuatl phonetics and morphology. Mariano Rojas, a native of Tepoztlán, in his *Manual de la lengua Nahuatl* (Mexico, 1927), lists Nahuatl names for many articles of European origin, but most of these, while intelligible, are the artificial constructs of a linguist, and few are in general use.

the imported traits found in Tepoztlán have entered
into this general culture. Some traits of material culture occur in Tepoztlán, particularly in houses near
the central *plaza*, which are not a part of the general
culture. Though perfectly familiar, they are possessed
only by individuals more used to modern city customs, and are regarded by the majority of the population as exterior to the common life. Features such
as these have not entered into the culture because too
expensive (brick floors; iron grilles) or because their
general acceptance would involve radical changes in
existing techniques (the fork). There is, therefore, a
classification which corresponds with subjective categories, between the integrated Tepoztecan culture, on
the one hand, and secondary, exterior elements, on the
other. These exterior elements are thought of as attributes of city life, that is, of modern industrial civilization. They are brought down to Tepoztlán by people used to city ways. When a Tepoztecan goes to the
city he to a certain extent temporarily assumes the
material culture of the metropolis. He has, not infrequently, a separate costume for city wear: dark trousers, a dark hat, and shoes, worn only on visits to the
city. This simple fact expresses the nature of the community of Tepoztlán: no longer a primitive tribal society nor yet an urbanized community, it must nevertheless be defined, as it tends to define itself, with reference to the world-wide city culture within which it
is now included.

The following table lists some features of the ma-

terial culture in columns representing the categories
suggested.

	GENERAL TEPOZTECAN CULTURE		SECONDARY ELEMENTS
Indian Elements	Mixed Elements	Spanish Elements	

MEN'S CLOTHING

Sandals	*Zarape*	Undergarments; shirt; trousers; vest; blouse; straw hat	Dark trousers; shoes; felt hat

WOMEN'S CLOTHING

(*Quechquemitl; pitzcueitl*)		The *rebozo* and almost all other clothing	Shoes

THE HOUSE

General form and materials: *Temazcal,* granaries; turkeys	Water-tank	Tiled roofs; hinged doors; chickens, pigs	Balconies; brick floor; iron grilles

HOUSE FURNISHINGS

Petate; otate bed; *tlequil; olla; metate; comal; molcajete; chiquihuite; tompiate*	*Cazuelas; jarros; bateas;* benches; stools	Table; candles; oilcans; water-carrier; *machete;* sewing machine	Brass bed; phonograph; oil lamp; forks Backed chairs; Brazier

FOODS AND STIMULANTS

Tortillas; moles; tamales; atoles: beans; maize; *chile;* squash; tomatoes, *pulque*	*Tortas;* tobacco	Bananas and citrus fruits; sugar; spices; rice; lima beans; beef and pork; chickens and eggs; coffee; *aguardiente*	Canned foods; beer

GENERAL TEPOZTECAN CULTURE			SECONDARY ELEMENTS
Indian Elements	Mixed Elements	Spanish Elements	

AGRICULTURE

Pointed stick	*Coa*	Plow	

TRANSPORT

Ayate; chiquihuite; *mecapal; huacal;* *bule*	*Morrales*	Horses; mules; *burros;* oxen	

MUSICAL INSTRUMENTS

Teponaztli	*Chirimía*	Guitar; cornet	Phonograph; violin

INDUSTRIES

Weaving; adobe- making		Brick- and tile- making; iron- working; car- pentering; shoemaking; breadmaking	Bottling drinks

CHAPTER III

THE ORGANIZATION OF THE COMMUNITY

In highly dissected regions the natural community tends to be the valley and the boundaries of the community are then the valley walls. Where the valley floor is wide and fertile a considerable village grows up. But also, in less desirable sites in the valley, in smaller pockets in the surrounding mountains, or on the steeper or less-watered slope on the other side of the mountains, settlements develop which, because of their relatively unfavorable locations, remain small. Upon the market and upon the social organization of the larger valley settlement the lesser hamlets become and remain dependent.

Such a constellation of minor settlements, tributary to a larger village, is exemplified by Tepoztlán and the seven hamlets of San Juanico, Santo Domingo, Amatlán, Ixcatepec, Santiago, San Andres, and Santa Catarina. Tepoztlán contains about four thousand inhabitants; the hamlets each hold two or three hundred. Tepoztlán lies in the wide valley that is protected by high mountain walls on three sides. It is well watered by many springs which burst forth from the mountains at the north side of the valley; this water is piped to the town (as once it was conducted through primitive stone conduits) from reservoirs built at these sources. Ixcatepec and Santiago are situated farther down the valley, outside the protecting walls, along the San Jerónimo, a tiny stream which arises in Tepoztlán and flows into the Rio Yautepec. The other five hamlets are almost or quite without immediate water; indeed, at Santa Catarina all water is carried to the town from a distance of about half a mile.

The small villages are naturally tributary to Tepoztlán because Tepoztlán is the large village to which they are nearest, but more particularly because most of them lie along the principal roads leading out of Tepoztlán. At the upper end of the valley, where the mountain wall is low, two roads go out: one north to Mexico City, the other southwest to Cuernavaca. San Juanico is situated on the former road; just off the latter road lies San Andres, and directly on it, Santa Catarina. The third road runs southeast down the widening valley to Yautepec. On this are situated Ixcatepec and Santiago. Santo Domingo and Amatlán lie on no main artery of travel, and for this reason they are much less definitely a part of the constellation of communities than are the other five. Much less often do the inhabitants of these two hamlets contribute to the market at Tepoztlán, or attend the *fiestas* there.

There is a great deal of travel among the villages of Morelos, and nearly all of it is travel on foot. A man or a woman of Tepoztlán will not infrequently make weekly trips, on foot, to Yautepec or to Cuernavaca, and will make the thirty-five or forty miles there and back in one day, often bearing a heavy load both

ways. Slow travel of this sort, with many rests, tends
to draw travelers who start out separately into little
groups. Particularly is this true on days of important
fiestas, when hundreds or thousands walk many miles
to and from the celebrating village, clustering for
gossip, exchanging news and opinions. Foot travel is
the newspaper of such regions.

The importance of foot travel is reflected in the conventional courtesies of the road. Not only is there, as
everywhere, a conventional greeting when two travelers meet face to face,[1] but also there is a conventional
greeting when one overtakes another. Where travel
is on foot, the moment of such passing is so prolonged
that the slight feeling of tension must be released by
means of a conventionalized greeting. So the traveler
overtaking another group says, *"Yenican anmuica,
amehuantzitzin"* ("Now here you go along, gentle-
men"), or may simply murmur *"Nican."* The others
reply, *"Quemacatzin, yenican tiatihue"* ("Yes, here we
go along"), or simply, *"Quemacatzin."* If the person
overtaking the others chooses not to join that group
but pushes on ahead he states that fact, saying,
"Mantiahtacan nepa ti nechnotzitzitzquilitin" ("We go
on, so as to get there"), generally shortened to *"Mantiahtacan."* The others give their assent or permission,
replying, *"Ximoica, nehua yolicniati"* ("Go ahead, I
go little by little").

In spite of the constant communication and inter-

---

[1] The greeting is, "Whither do you go?"—"*Adonde van?*" in a Spanish context and "*Canin anmuica?*" in a Nahuatl context.

action which is implied by such frequent travel, the villages composing this natural community remain separate and individual. The social intercourse of five hundred years or more has not destroyed the cultural peculiarities of each hamlet. This is because a change of residence is not common. Among the men of Tepoztlán very few—a guess would suggest fifty—were born outside the valley. More of the women are from other parts of Mexico. And even among the villages composing the community there is infrequent migration. The inhabitants cling closely to their ancestral lands. During part of the past period of revolution (1910–17) Tepoztlán was deserted; many of the houses were destroyed; yet when peace came most of the population returned, each family again to occupy the same housesite, to cultivate the same *milpa*, as they and their fathers had before.

Some of the cultural differences between villages have their origin in geographic differences. The most important concept of direction in Tepoztlán has to do with altitude. As in Polynesian islands where directions are not given in terms of the compass points but rather as "toward the sea" or "away from the sea," so in Tepoztlán a location with reference to the speaker is not usually given in terms of north, south, east, or west but is instead described as "down below" or "a little way above." The general appearance of the hamlet of San Juanico differs markedly from that of Tepoztlán. The two are no more than four miles apart, but one is two thousand feet above the other.

Therefore the flora is different; and furthermore the soil is not suitable for *adobe*, so that most of the houses are of cane, straw, or wattle.

Differences in altitude and in aridity produce differences in the sorts of natural products of these eight villages; thus it comes about that villages have agricultural and economic specialties. San Juanico furnishes *tejocotes* (*manzanillas*), and a variety of medicinal herbs which grow only at a high altitude. San Andres, situated on a limestone ridge, contributes the lime, burned in its kilns, in which all maize is cooked. Santiago is a warmer and better-watered village than the others, and its inhabitants supply tomatoes, sugar cane, and sapotes. The people of Ixcatepec specialize in honey, and those of arid Santa Catarina often bring acacia pods (S. *guajes;* N. *huexi*).

This economic specialization facilitates exchange at the bi-weekly market. Every Wednesday and every Sunday morning fifty to a hundred vendors gather in the central *plaza* of Tepoztlán. Some of these are from Tepoztlán itself, some from the tributary hamlets, and a few from villages outside the community. The merchant simply squats on his heels on the *plaza*, or under the *portales* in front of the permanent shops, or he may sit on a stone, displaying his wares in little piles. For the privilege of occupying such a space the municipal government exacts a "floor tax" (*derecho de piso*). The positions taken by the merchants do not vary substantially from week to week, nor, indeed, from generation to generation; those from each surrounding hamlet sit always together, and always in the same absolute and relative position. The merchants come by villages, and sit by villages; and the differences between them are further emphasized by the fact that the products they sell are largely different, as one village group is compared with another. There is thus the following permanent market pattern:

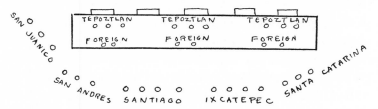

Amatlán also has an economic specialty: the making of beds of cane;[1] but Amatlán and Santo Domingo, as has already been stated, are less firmly associated with the rest of the valley community, and their inhabitants do not regularly bring goods to sell at the market.

⟨Differences between the villages are not limited to those brought about by geographic factors. The stability of populations, even within the small confines of this natural community, and the local nature of traditional loyalties, have made it possible for other cultural distinctions to survive. Outside of the Tepoztlán community, such differences are, of course, more marked. Yautepec is no more than fifteen miles away, but a native of Tepoztlán may tell a traveler coming

[1] Not verified by personal observation.

from Yautepec at a considerable distance because he
wears his trousers shorter and tighter and because he
is likely to wear a handkerchief at his neck. It is also
probable that there are dialectic differences[1] which
distinguish Yautepec from Tepoztlán. Of differences
between hamlets within the community there are
probably many. In Santa Catarina beans are first
toasted and then boiled with much *epazote*,[2] whereas
in Tepoztlán that staple is not toasted and the boiling
is usually without *epazote*. No statistical proof can be
offered here of the statement, which in Tepoztlán is
generally accepted as representing the fact, that in
San Andres marriage takes place, "according to ancient custom," generally at the age of twelve to sixteen, whereas in Tepoztlán the ages are most commonly from eighteen to twenty-four.

In spite of local differences, the eight villages are
bound together by certain institutions in which each
village has a share. Chief of these institutions are the
common lands, the market, and the traditional festal
and ceremonial organization. The bi-weekly interchange of goods and gossip at the market has already
been briefly described. The other two principal inte-
grating factors require more comment.

The common lands[3] of the community constitute

---

[1] Differences in Spanish spoken. Little Nahuatl is spoken at Yautepec, which,
although a pre-Columbian site, is now largely a *mestizo* community.

[2] *Chenopodium ambrosioides* L. This statement rests on the account of one
informant.

[3] The general subject of "The Land Systems of Mexico" is admirably treated
in G. M. McBride's book of that title, previously cited.

probably the strongest single factor operating to draw the eight villages together. The lands were thus influential in pre-Columbian times when all real property was held in common, usually not by the *pueblo* but by the subdivision of the *pueblo*, the *calpolli*.[1] Since the Reforma (1857) communal holdings have been generally reduced to individual tenure. This was probably early accomplished in Tepoztlán; private agricultural tracts are there the subject of entirely individual ownership and sale. Nevertheless the private lands are encircled by public lands in which all inhabitants of the eight villages share and which, with the *milpas*, constitute the local "fatherland."

There are thus both private and public lands in Tepoztlán. The private lands include:

1. *House sites (sitios) with their attendant agricultural plots (milpas).*—Characteristically each *sitio* has an appendant *milpa*, which may be located as much as a mile away from the *sitio;* but the two are usually taxed, and inherited together. These tracts are not infrequently sold, but most of them have been in the same family for many generations. Most of the produce supporting the community is raised on the *milpas*. There should also be mentioned the *corrales*, yards at the back of dwellings sometimes planted with corn or beans.

2. *Milpas de labor.*—These are agricultural lands reduced to private possession and tillage out of the

---

[1] The *calpolli* was perhaps originally a kinship unit; its limited survival in Tepoztlán will be discussed in a subsequent chapter.

public lands, whether *cerriles* or *pastales*. Anyone (first obtaining permission from the municipal authorities) may till such an unoccupied piece. The inhabitants of the seven hamlets and of Tepoztlán stand on equal footing with regard to this privilege. Once the tract is reduced to possession trespass or theft is punished. The right to cultivate tracts such as these is probably sometimes sold, but no permanent title ever vests, because if the occupant fails to cultivate his tract, the municipality may reassign the tract. It is, therefore, perhaps strictly incorrect to include these lands among private holdings. But the cultivator speaks of the land as his, and, as has been said, he may even sell what right he has.

3. *Tlacololli.*—What has been said with regard to the *milpas de labor* as to tenure and cultivation applies equally to *tlacololli*. They differ only in that the former often embrace considerable areas, and are like separate farms (*ranchitas*), and they may be cultivated year after year; while the latter are small tracts of cleared land on steep mountain sides (they are taken out of the public *cerriles*). As the soil, once cleared, quickly washes away, they may be tilled no more than one or a few seasons.[1]

The public lands are those wide tracts of land unsuitable for agriculture which surround the private *milpas*. They are of two sorts: pasture lands on arid slopes (*pastales*) and wooded mountain sides (*cerriles*). They represent, historically, that part of the com-

[1] "I will open for you a *tlaculol*," sings the lover to his lady in a local ballad.

munal lands of the Indian *pueblo*, the *altepetlalli*, which has not been converted to private holdings, and they equally represent the communal pastures and wood lots of the medieval Spanish village.[1] Together, *pastales* and *cerriles* constitute the *ejido* of the present *pueblo*. Anyone from Tepoztlán or the seven hamlets may pasture cattle or cut wood in these lands.[2] These common lands are a source of frequent discussion and dispute; regulations are made for their protection and administration and often they are the subject of quarrels with neighboring landholding units. For many years Tepoztlán (the entire municipality) has disputed with the *hacienda* of Oacalco the ownership to certain marginal lands, and the fact that the *hacienda* is now not in private hands but in the hands of the state has not abated the quarrel.

Such a dispute, of the entire valley community with another landholding organization, serves to enhance the local *esprit de corps*. But it must be said that land disputes may operate to set one village against another as well as to draw them all together. It is probable that not infrequently one village comes to claim a special right in some particular part of the *ejido*. In 1927 a dispute developed with regard to certain mountain lands in which the inhabitants of Santa Catarina were cutting wood for charcoal without first

[1] McBride, *Land Systems of Mexico*, p. 114.

These public lands, it will be observed, are exploited by individuals for private profit. The only lands in Tepoztlán which are both communally owned and communally operated for communal profit are the lands belonging to the local chapels; these will be explained in a later chapter.

obtaining the permission of the municipal authorities in Tepoztlán. The land had once belonged to another neighboring *hacienda* and had been the subject of another prolonged dispute in the course of which lives were taken, but for some time now the *hacienda* has been a ruin and a memory. Tepoztlán claims to have purchased the land, through the form of a conveyance to a group of citizens, while Santa Catarina denies this sale and claims to have made a contract with the *hacienda* granting permission to cut wood on the property. When the local government arrested the *carboneros* of Santa Catarina, that hamlet asserted its alleged special rights with vigor, and a considerable bitterness developed between the people of Tepoztlán and those of Santa Catarina.

The eight villages are in this manner bound into a community by common interests which stimulate now co-operation, now competition. The same alternation of opposing tendencies—one centripetal, one centrifugal—can be observed in connection with the institutions which carry on the social and ceremonial activities. Each village is under the protection of the local saint whose image is housed in the single church of the village. On the name day of the saint the village holds a *fiesta* celebrating this patron god. These occasions require a great deal of preparation involving food for the festal dishes, decoration of the church, fireworks, religious dances, etc. The village is then the focus of attention for the people of the community; and to the *fiesta* come also many from outside the valley. As will be later explained in more detail in connection with the *fiestas* of the *barrios*, these *fiestas* render expressive the *esprit de corps* of the villages. A strong feeling of group solidarity develops, and not a little feeling of competition, each village priding itself on the merits of its *santo* and the splendor of its *fiesta*.

At the same time a traditional pattern of co-operation among villages unites them as against mere visitors from outside the valley. On the occasion of very important *fiestas*, given in small hamlets, as, for example, the annual *fiesta* of Ixcatepec, the *mayordomos* charged with the care of the *santos* in Tepoztlán and the neighboring villages meet and agree to distribute the burden of an eight-day *fiesta* among the group. Each *mayordomo* then becomes responsible for one day for the care of the *santo* of Ixcatepec, and undertakes to provide the candles burned that day. Everyone from Tepoztlán goes to Ixcatepec, and the *fiesta* is thought of as a *fiesta* of the whole community. The cockfights attending the *fiesta* of Ixcatepec may then be held as Tepoztlán *vs.* Cuernavaca, or Tepoztlán *vs.* Yautepec.

Such institutions integrate into a single community a number of more or less independent villages with special cultures and traditions. The term for "countryman" (*paisano*) more often than not means an inhabitant of Tepoztlán or one of the satellite villages, and will not be applied to a man from outside the immediate valley.

It remains to indicate the relation of the formal government to the actual social organization. The local political unit, the *municipalidad*, embraces Tepoztlán and the seven satellite hamlets and is therefore a recognition of the natural community. The seat of municipal government is at Tepoztlán. It consists of a municipal council (*consejo municipal*), embracing one chief officer (*presidente*) and eight assistants (*ayudantes*), a secretary, and a judge (*juez*). The last, with the aid of a more literate secretary, hears local complaints, and, if he cannot compose them, transmits memoranda on such matters to Cuernavaca. The government is in form elected annually on the first of January. In fact, it is (at the time of this study) appointed from Cuernavaca, the seat of the state government, from among those in political sympathy with the state government in power.[1] At present,[2] election by viva voce, as an emergency measure, under control of the party in power, permits a slate to be installed with the active participation of a handful of adherents and the almost complete indifference of the body of the population.

This government does little beyond the administration of routine matters. Except for occasional regulations dealing with the exploitation of or possible injury to the communal lands, no legislation is passed. An attempt is made to collect local taxes,[3] but such

[1] During 1927 the Campesinos (rural radical party).

[2] 1927.

[3] There are four: a tax on real estate, a sales tax on domestic animals, a tax for use of the slaughter-house, and the tax on merchants using the public *plaza*.

attempts are not infrequently resented by individuals who paid no taxes during the years of the revolution. Furthermore, valuation of property is in the hands of a committee of inhabitants who put down their own and their neighbors' lands for a merely nominal value. Thus deprived of revenues, the municipal government cannot initiate improvements.

Until recent years local government was by the old *cacique* system whereby a single individual of personality and local prestige ruled the community with the consent of public opinion. The *cacique* usually served for life. This system, along with the informal neighborhood organizations to be described later, probably suited better the political spirit of the village than do the exterior forms of an annually elected and annually changed municipal board. Now the law is enforced requiring the municipal government to be changed every year.

Nevertheless this government, drawn from the people, more nearly represents them than did the provisional rulers sent down after the revolution by the federal government, or than do now the collectors of the state tax, where they are outsiders similarly imposed on the community by the state. Such proconsular representatives of an exterior power remain, so far as personal experience would indicate, only long enough to exploit and defraud the natives. Justly the objects of fear and suspicion, they pass a tenure of office in no small measure dependent on the readiness of the gun.

Disregarding such occasional foreigners in the political personnel, one may say that the municipal council is expressive rather than active. It maintains prestige, presides at public meetings, and receives the sal-
utations of visitors. Actual work, as, for example, the
installation of a lamp in the *plaza*, the exploitation of
marketable wild roots on the public lands, or the pro-
motion of the secular celebrations, is done by the
small group of townspeople who are richer, better
educated, and more accustomed to city ways than
others. These men are the shopkeepers and many of
the artisans. They are *los correctos*—the "correct"
people—as contrasted with *los tontos*[1]—the "ignorant"
people. The former wear shoes and dark trousers; the
latter, sandals and white trousers. The personnel of
the municipal government now tends to be drawn
from *los tontos*, while *los correctos* constitute the influential citizens who occupy the other half of the
platform at public meetings but who regard politics
with something akin to disdain. Politics, therefore, is
enjoyed by the same element in the population that
organizes the religious *fiestas*, and, like these, constitutes a form of play.

[1] It may be stated, perhaps unnecessarily, that these two terms (*tontos* and
correctos) are used in the following pages not in their original Spanish meanings,
but merely to designate two groups in Tepoztlán that are sometimes so designated by the people themselves, and that lack other convenient names.

CHAPTER IV

THE ORGANIZATION OF THE VILLAGE

The social organization of the village itself follows
the same pattern as that just described for the entire
valley community. Tepoztlán, like the whole community of which it is the largest village, is made up of
semi-independent units, each of which centers about
a church and a patron saint. These units are the *barrios*. The *barrios* are the contiguous component parts
of the village, but their presence and relative positions are indicated by the towers of the seven small
churches or chapels (*capillas*) which, with the great
central church situated on the *plaza*, alone of the
buildings of Tepoztlán, project above the sea of foliage which covers the town in the rainy season. These
seven small chapels are scattered about the village;
no two are close together. Each is located in and is
the property of one of the seven *barrios*. The chapel
and the *barrio* take their name from the saint whose
image is placed on the altar of the chapel and on
whose name day falls the *fiesta* of that *barrio*. Santa
Cruz has not one, but two, *fiestas*—one on May 3, the
other on August 6—because there are two images in
the chapel, that of the Santa Cruz and that of San
Salvador. In this case, while the *barrio* is known as
Santa Cruz, Saint Salvador[1] is thought of as the pat-

[1] "Saint Salvador"—rather than an aspect of the Christ.

ron of the *barrio*. The small hamlet of Ixcatepec, just
outside Tepoztlán, has the same two images and the
same two *fiestas*. By arrangement of long standing,
however, Ixcatepec celebrates its *fiestas* a week after
those of Santa Cruz.

The *barrios* vary a great deal in size. The number of
houses in each *barrio* is approximately as follows:

San Pedro	35	La Santísima (Trinidad).	175
Los Reyes	65	San Miguel	150
San Sebastian	14	San Domingo	175
Santa Cruz	100		

Roughly speaking, there are four large *barrios* and
three small ones. The three large *barrios* last named
are grouped about the central *plaza*, while the three
small ones and Santa Cruz are situated above (west
of) the others.[1] The boundaries of the *barrios* are
clearly defined. Sometimes a boundary runs in the
middle of a street and sometimes the houses on both
sides pertain to the same *barrio*, the boundary then running just behind a row of houses. Occasionally there are
irregular jogs which take a few houses out of a block
and include them in another *barrio*. A whole block of
houses, geographically in San Miguel, belong to the
barrio of Santa Cruz, although almost at the opposite
end of town.[2] The inhabitants of these houses take
their turn in the care of the chapel of Santa Cruz, and
pay the contribution paid by *barrio* members at the
time of the *fiesta* of that *barrio*.

[1] See map, p. 220.

[2] How this came about the writer is unable to say. No informant had any
explanation.

It is clear that topographic factors have been of some significance in fixing *barrio* boundaries. In many cases there is now a *barranca* or a sudden declivity where one *barrio* ends and another begins. This is especially notable in the cases of the boundaries between San Pedro and Los Reyes, Los Reyes and Santa Cruz, Los Reyes and San Sebastian, La Santísima and Santo Domingo. Tepoztlán, it has already been observed, is situated on a steep slope, and the *barrios* occur in the order previously given from the upper end of the slope to the lower. If one looks at the town from the mountains on the south side of the valley, the seven chapels appear in a ranking series, one above another. This relation may be indicated in the following diagram. San Miguel extends over two levels.

San Pedro
   Los Reyes
      San Sebastian
      and Santa Cruz
         La Santísima
         and San Miguel
            San Miguel and
            Santo Domingo

It is worthy of note that those pairs of *barrios* which occur at the same level resemble one another in cultural features more than other pairs. Thus, San Sebastian and Santa Cruz have special similarities in occupations and religious sentiments and bear the same animal appellation (as will be later explained); while in the case of San Miguel and La Santísima one of the principal streets runs continuously on the same level through the two *barrios* and the pair are much alike and co-operate for the carnival and for other *fiestas*.

The Tepoztecos are conscious of the part played by these geographic features. During an annual *fiesta* an actor impersonating their eponymous "king," El Te-pozteco, recites a traditional rôle in Nahuatl in the course of which, as he is defying the besieging armies of other neighboring villages, he says, "*Ica hueloncan nechmoyohualotica nahui no tepe, chicome tlatelli, chi-come tlacomolli, ihuan chicome tlaltemimilolli*" ("Here I am surrounded by my four mountains, seven hills, seven wells and seven stony hillsides"). This is clearly a reference, in topographic terms, to the *barrios*.

The word *barrio* is frequently translated "ward," but "ward" does not correctly suggest the nature of the unit. In the first place the *barrio* is not a political unit. For purposes of municipal government the town has been divided into seven *demarcaciónes*. It is plain that the *barrios* have been the general pattern for the creation of the *demarcaciónes*, but the boundaries of the two sets of units do not coincide. People do not know what *demarcación* they live in; many are prob-ably ignorant that such an artificial unit exists. In the second place, while one becomes a member of a "ward," as we know it, merely by going and living in that area, one may not in this way become a member of a *barrio*. Membership in the *barrio* is, generally speaking, hereditary. In most cases people live on the sites in which lived their ancestors for many generations. These house sites bear individual Nahuatl names[1] by which addresses are given; street names are rarely used. When, therefore, an individual comes from without a *barrio* and rents a house there, he does not thereby become a member of that *barrio*. Lists given of *barrio* members often omit the occupants of certain houses, and these always turn out to be houses rented by outsiders, or, in a few cases, houses owned and occupied by members of other *barrios*.

This latter case leads to the point that there are living in every *barrio* certain families that are known to belong to a *barrio* other than that in which they live.[2] This probably came about when an ancestor bought a site in some other *barrio*. In these cases the entire family must have moved, leaving no one in the old *barrio* to continue the membership there. Of course a man may and probably frequently does change his *barrio* membership by changing his *barrio* residence. This may come about if a father with several sons buys for one or more of them a house site in another *barrio*. The son, usually the oldest, who re-

---

[1] Such names are: *Totoc*, "place of birds"; *Tlateliticpac*, "on top of the slope"; *Tecuantlan*, "place of wolves"; *Tlaxcalchican*, "place of *tortillas*"; *Techichilco*, "red stone"; *Iztapa*, "place of salt"; *Teopanixpa*, "in front of the church." Some are hybrid terms, as: *Pulquetlan*, "place of pulque"; *Cruznepanihyan*, "place of crossed crosses." A typical contemporary Nahuatl toponomy is to be found in Gamio, *La población del valle de San Juan Teotihuacan*, Tomo II, Vol. II, pp. 649 ff.

[2] One of the writer's informants, living in Los Reyes, belonged to La Santísima, although neither she nor any other informant could tell at what time the family had moved. In Los Reyes there are five families from La Santísima, two from San Miguel, and three from Santa Cruz.

mains in the old *barrio* carries on after his father's death the membership in the old *barrio* and fulfils the pledge to that *santo*, while the younger son takes up membership in another *barrio*. It will be observed that there is a tendency for the men within a *barrio* to be related rather than the women, because in most cases a married son brings his wife to live in his father's house, or in a new house built on or near the same house site, while daughters marry and often go to live in other *barrios*. The *barrio* probably in no way affects the choice of spouse; no influences on such choice appear except influences of propinquity and temperamental preference.

Membership in the *barrio* is attested by the important fact of payment of the offering (S. *limosna*; N. *huentli*) at the time of the *fiesta* of the *santo* of the *barrio*, and it is so perpetuated in the cases of individuals belonging to *barrios* other than those in which they live. Thus the La Santísima families in Los Reyes pay the offering when the *fiesta* of La Santísima takes place. They may also pay the offering for the *fiesta* of Los Reyes, but this is recognized as a later obligation and does not cancel membership in the *barrio* of La Santísima. By this same ceremonial payment the fact that the people living in the Santa Cruz enclave within San Miguel belong to Santa Cruz is annually revived at the *fiesta* of Santa Cruz. The offering is thought of as a perpetual pledge to the *santo*, irrevocable, and binding on a man's family after his death. The money so paid is expended for one or both of two purposes: the candles burned before the *santo* on the day of the *fiesta*, and the tower of fireworks (*castillo*) burned in the atrium of the church on that occasion. The payment for each of these purposes, of the year's instalment of the perpetual pledge, is an occasion attended by solemnizing ritual, both acted and spoken. The ceremonies take place at the houses of the *mayordomos* of the candles and of the *castillo*, and the occasions are known respectively as the *cerahpa* and the *castiyohpa*.[1]

As has already been indicated in a previous chapter, the *ejidos* of Tepoztlán are not, as were the *altepetlalli* of the pre-Columbian town, divided into sections among the *barrios*. The pastures and wood lots belonging to the town are used in common by all the *pueblo* (and by the seven smaller villages) without regard to *barrio* membership. The private agricultural fields are not grouped according to *barrios*. A resident of San Miguel may own a *milpa* over near Santa Cruz at the other side of town, although as a matter of fact *milpas* are, naturally, more often than not situated near the owner's dwelling.

But each *barrio* owns lands the produce of which goes to the support of the chapel of the *barrio*. Or, as the Tepoztecans would put it, the produce goes to the support of the *santo*. The lands are referred to as *imimil to santo*, "the *milpas* of our *santo*." These are the only truly communal lands of Tepoztlán. Conform-

---

[1] This ritual is briefly described on p. 100, and more fully in Redfield, art., "The Cerahpa and the Castiyohpa in Tepoztlan."

able with law, the legal title to these lands is held by an individual, but he holds in trust for the *santo*. His interest in the land is no greater than that of any other member of the *barrio*. The lands are sowed, tended, and harvested in common by the men of the *barrio*, under the direction of the *mayordomo* of the *santo*, and the crop, when sold, goes to the upkeep of the chapel—for candles, curtains for the altars, etc. Most of the lands so communally owned by the *barrios* are *milpas* on which maize is grown. But San Miguel also owns a grove of *chirimoyas*, and San Pedro owns a grove of cedars. (Cedar boughs, now as in pre-Columbian times, are much used in decorating altars and are subject to other religious and magical uses.) In addition, certain of the *barrios*, notably San Miguel, own bulls which are used for *toros*, a sort of rustic bullfight sometimes held on the occasion of the *fiesta* of the *santo*. During the rest of the year the bulls are loaned out to members of the *barrio* for upkeep.[1]

The *barrio* is plainly recognizable as the pre-Columbian *calpolli*. From the accounts[2] we have of the social organization of Tenochtitlan (Mexico City) and of Texcoco, it appears that each *pueblo* in the Nahua area was divided into units which bore this name. These units were originally, it has been supposed,[3]

[1] The communal ownership of these bulls is not fully attested. During the year of the writer's stay San Miguel lent its bulls to Los Reyes at the time of the *fiesta* of the latter *barrio;* Los Reyes had none of its own, or too few.

[2] See T. T. Waterman, *Bandelier's Contribution to the Study of Ancient Mexican Social Organization.*

[3] *Ibid.* Spinden, *Ancient Civilizations of Mexico and Central America,* p. 190, contra.

based on kinship, but at the time of the Conquest, in Tenochtitlan at least, the kinship tie had largely disappeared, and the *calpolli* was a local unit. Each had its own god, religious structure, courts and judges, and military organization; and the members of each *calpolli* owned in common lands apart and distinct from the lands of the other *calpolli*.

With the destruction of the tribal organization following the Conquest, the military, political, and judicial functions of the *calpolli* fell into desuetude. But the social and religious functions, conflicting with none of the Spanish forms, and coinciding in some measure with the current Spanish notion of a church parish, continued in Tepoztlán, as no doubt in other *pueblos*, to this day. The *barrio* as a religious organization, the central religious building, the patron-god whose image is contained within it,[1] and elements in the accompanying ceremonial (e.g., the *teponaztli*, offering of flower garlands, *copal* incense, etc.) are survivals from pre-Columbian culture.

It is in the social and festal organization of the community that the *barrio* maintains its importance. Even when there is no *fiesta* the chapel serves as a sort of social center for the *barrio;* the water tank is generally there and near it people congregate to gossip. Some of the *barrios* have purchased gasoline

[1] In the commentary to the Codex Magliabecchi, sec. 62, it is stated: "Each barrio has another idol. They say it was he who guarded the barrio. To him they run with their petitions in times of necessity. On the day on which the festival of this idol falls, the people of the barrio offer him solemnities. The other barrios do not." This is precisely the situation in Tepoztlán today.

lamps which are hung in the street outside the chapel, and here the youths of the *barrio* come in the evening to talk, gamble, or listen to songs. But it is at the time of the annual *fiesta* that the collective importance of the *barrio* members reaches its highest importance, and the chapel becomes the great focus of interest for the entire *pueblo* and even for neighboring villages. The decoration of the chapel, the ceremonial bringing of the candles, the burning of the candles, the erection and burning of the *castillo*, the preparation and consumption of the festal dishes, the playing of the ancient flute or the *teponaztli* on the roof of the chapel, one or more sacred dances and sometimes *toros*—all constitute a program of ritual and entertainment which occupies from one to seven days. Although members of other *barrios* take part in the entertainment, the *barrio* whose *santo* is celebrated acts as host, and its members very much feel their collective importance.

The *santo* is the symbol of the collective spirit of the *barrio*. It is not uncommon for an individual to boast of the superior miraculousness of the *santo* of his *barrio*: "Our *barrio* is the most important because our image is the most miraculous." San Salvador protected the people of Santa Cruz during the revolution; San Sebastian appears in dreams to the people of his *barrio*, and offers them advice, etc.

There is, therefore, a morale, an *esprit de corps*, inhering in the *barrio*, embodied in the *santo* and occasionally expressed as rivalry. Every exertion must be expended on the *fiesta* to maintain the *barrio* prestige. The organizations which support the carnival, a secular *fiesta*, are creations of three of these *barrios*. These three *comparsas* (groups of men organizing masked "leaping") strive each to make a better show, offer a larger orchestra than do the others, and as a consequence disputes not infrequently arise.[1]

It is not too much to say that the members of a *barrio* tend to think and act alike. In very large measure this is because of the unifying and centralizing influence of the chapel and its *santo*, with the attendant co-operative work and play. A group of men of the *barrio* together prepare the *milpa* of the *santo* for sowing, together hoe the growing maize, together gather the harvest. A group of women of the *barrio* together prepare the food for the men so employed in the fields. In the former cases the work is done under the direction of the steward (*mayordomo*) of the *santo*. His wife, or the principal woman of his household, organizes the cooking of *tortillas*, beans, and meat.

In some instances there are economic factors which enforce this collective sentiment. Thus, what charcoal is burned in Tepoztlán is nearly all burned in San Pedro, and, to a less extent, in Los Reyes. The members of these *barrios*, in cutting, hauling, and burning

---

[1] During the year of the writer's stay trouble between Santo Domingo and San Miguel was only averted by an arrangement that the two *comparsas* were to "leap" on different days. As has been pointed out, the competitive spirit does not prevent *mayordomos* of *barrios* and villages from co-operating for important *fiestas*.

wood, are drawn together by their common occupation. More marked is the part played by the twisting of ropes of maguey fiber among the inhabitants of San Sebastian. This industry, introduced a generation ago by an emigrant to Tepoztlán, has spread to few houses outside of the *barrio* in which he settled; but in San Sebastian almost every household is so occupied, and when there is an important fair in some larger town in the state, the men of San Sebastian will go there almost in a body to market their lassos and *riatas*.

The *barrios* have, indeed, obviously different cultures, or, what is the same thing, different personalities. The varying characteristics of the *barrios* are recognized by the Tepoztecos themselves, and at least the more reflective of them can express the differences they feel. Thus, Santo Domingo is the most civilized *barrio*, and the most patriotic (i.e., most nearly conscious of national feeling). Their chapel is decorated with Mexican flags; a modern orchestra was organized here, etc. Santa Cruz is strongly primitive—Catholic, exclusive, and independent—"Santa Cruz governs itself like a little republic." San Pedro is a *barrio* of poor, illiterate people who preserve to a marked extent ancient mentality and resent the presence of outsiders in their midst, etc.

The consciousness of *barrio* personalities receives an expression in names which are applied to the *barrios*. These names are in Nahuatl and are in every case the names of animals. The names are:

Santo Domingo......*Cacame* ["Toads"]
La Santísima........*Tzicame* ["Ants"]
San Miguel..........*Techihehicame* ["Lizards"]
Santa Cruz and
    San Sebastian.....*Tepemaxtlame* ["Cacomixtles"]*
Los Reyes..........*Metzalcuanime* ["Maguey
                             worms"]
San Pedro..........*Tlacuatzitzin* ["Tlacuaches"]†

* The bassarisk (*Bassariscus astutus*).
† The opossum (*Didelphys marsupialis*).

These names are used, somewhat humorously, to refer to the members of the *barrio* considered collectively. Thus, as the saint day of Santo Domingo, January 12, approaches, it will be said: "*Ye acitihuitz ilhuitl cacame*" ("Now comes the *fiesta* of the toads").

There are two explanations offered by the Tepoztecos for these names. The first explanation says that the animal named is one which is particularly common at the time when the *fiesta* of that *barrio* is held. Thus, the *fiesta* of La Santísima is in June when the *milpas* are plowed for sowing and many ants appear on the ground; that of Santa Cruz in May when the cacomixtles come down to eat the sapotes which are ripe at that time and falling to the ground; that of Los Reyes in January when the maguey is opened for pulque and the worms come to eat the exposed pulp. The other explanation, which is more common, declares that the names are descriptive of the characteristics of the *barrio* members. The people of La Santísima are called ants because there are so many of them; they run over the ground like ants and get into all sorts of affairs. Those of Santo Domingo are called toads not only because they live nearest the water, but because they swell so with their own importance. Those of San Miguel are called lizards because they are so quick (*lijero*) and light minded, liking to play and sing so much at night on the street corners. Those of Santa Cruz are called cacomixtles because they live up under the rocks with the cacomixtles. These characterizations are certainly apt. It is doubtful if they represent modifications of pre-Columbian names of *calpolli*. Similar collective designations, though not always in Nahuatl and not usually animal terms, are found in other Mexican villages.[1] But the names do represent the consciousness of *barrio* individualities and help to show how Tepoztlán is a federation of semi-independent units, as was no doubt the pre-Columbian *pueblo*.

[1] Gamio, *op. cit.*, Tomo II, Vol. II, p. 402.

CHAPTER V

THE RHYTHMS OF THE SOCIAL LIFE

En outre, ni l'individu, ni la société, ne sont indépendants de la nature, de l'univers, lequel est lui aussi soumis à des rythmes qui ont leur contre-coup sur la vie humaine. Dans l'univers aussi, il y a des étapes et des moments de passage, des marches en avant et des stades d'arrêt relatif, de suspension [Arnold Van Gennep, *Les rites de passage*, p. 4].

In Tepoztlán, as in other simple societies, the pulse of life is measured more directly than it is with us by the great clocks of the sky. Life everywhere is not a sustained adjustment, but a series of crises and lyses, an alternation of tension and release. The movement of this rhythm is set in the first instance by astronomical recurrences. The rotation of the earth, the revolution of the earth around the sun, even the waxing and waning of the moon, constitute the metronome of human interests. Upon these cadences of nature the simpler peoples are more directly dependent. Elsewhere artificial heat and light, and the interchange of products of different climates, go far toward making one hour, or day, or month, like another. But, while in Tepoztlán the clock in the tower of the Palacio Municipal strikes the hours, the sound of its bell reaches the ears of a small number of the inhabitants, and all are far more attentive to the chronometers of sunset and sunrise, and of wet season and dry.

83

For this reason one hour of daylight is as good as another, and it does not matter at precisely what time a thing is done. An "appointment" is too sharp a concept for a people moving with the more deliberate cycles of the stars. "It will take place right now, at about three or five o'clock," a Tepoztecan may say shortly after noon. On the other hand, because the rhythms of the group activity change almost completely with the changes of the season, the months within the year are individual, unique, each with its appropriate festivals, to be anticipated and at last enjoyed. The next year again repeats the sequence and the cadence of the last. Only the irregular occurrence of war breaks up the rhythm of the years and brings about a longer cycle of activity: a slow crescendo of restoration, of anabolism, after sudden catastrophe.

The daily rhythm of the Tepoztlán man, as contrasted with that of the woman, is more dependent upon the alternation of night and day. Chiefly he works in the fields, or in other outdoor activities (as *arriero*, for example, transporting goods from the railroad to the storekeepers in Tepoztlán), where nightfall ends his labors. A comparatively small number of individuals, those employed in the municipal government, perhaps the storekeepers and a few others, follow a daily schedule dependent upon clocks and watches, and pursue much the same activity throughout the year. But most of the men leave the fields only when the day is over during the busy agricultural seasons, while at other times of the year they may be largely or wholly idle.

The daily cycle of activity of the woman, on the other hand, follows much the same course throughout the year, but is not so clearly ended each day by the coming of darkness. While he is led by the cycle of the sun, she is the servant of another cycle—that of hunger and its satisfaction. The woman's practical activities are organized around the preparation of food. Grinding and cooking, she is engaged most of the hours of the day and many of the night. The man fetches wood for the hearth from the mountains, and brings most of the water used from the nearest tank; the rest of the domestic economy is in the hands of the woman.

The day begins while yet the sun is below the horizon. At once five hundred or more fires are kindled by the women of Tepoztlán; the acrid, low-clinging smoke of the pitch-pine kindling rises from the valley. The housewife begins at once to grind maize for the morning *tortillas* and to cook the breakfast dishes. Usually three meals are taken, one at about seven or eight o'clock, another an hour or more after noon, and a third at seven or eight at night. Some people, for whom the night is cool and the bed hard, stir themselves once during the night to eat once more before returning to rest.[1] At every meal *tortillas* are eaten. If times are bad, there may be only beans besides, or perhaps not even beans. When meat is obtainable, it

[1] This is hearsay.

is usually prepared as *clemole*, boiled and served with a sauce of *chiles*. This is a favorite breakfast dish. The wealthier and more sophisticated buy baker's bread for the morning and the evening meals, but eat *tortillas* too. The afternoon meal is much the same; it is likely to be the heaviest meal of the day. Then may be eaten lima beans toasted, or *tortas*, or perhaps chick-peas. Coffee or chocolate, and less commonly milk, may be drunk at any meal.

Intimately, when only the family is present, all sit together on the ground beside the hearth and eat. (Of course the well-to-do use tables.) If male company is present, the man sits with the guests and they are served by his wife, who eats alone. After breakfast the man goes to the field, or to his workbench; the wife resumes her domestic labors. The last sound at night, when all other sounds but the braying of *burros* and the barking of dogs have failed, is the slap-slap of the *tortillera* and the subdued, wet, rubbing sound of the maize-grinder.

A large share of the woman's life and interests is taken up with the *metate*, that ancient grinding-stone that has not changed in form or function for thousands of years. For some ten years a small steam mill has been in operation in Tepoztlán;[1] to this the women may bring their maize to be ground. But that most of the maize is, nevertheless, ground on domestic *metates* is due not only to the fact that mill-ground maize

[1] This is owned and operated not by a Tepoztecan but by a man from Xochimilco, Federal District.

is more expensive, but to the fact that a woman's status (except among the few sophisticated) is determined in no small degree by her skill and industry at the grinding-stone. She takes pride in her grinding. Differences in skill are tasted in the finished *tortilla;* men even claim to identify the grinding of their wives in the *tortilla* they eat. A woman known to be incompetent or negligent at the *metate* is not a desirable wife.[1] One of the diseases recognized in Tepoztlán is *tlancuatlatzihuiztli*, "laziness of the knees." The swelling of the knees which signalizes this affliction is due, not to too much grinding, but to too little; it is thus shown that the sufferer has neglected her work. A woman grinds two or three times a day. On ordinary days the grinding for an average household requires about six hours. But if the men of the household are to go away to work on some distant *hacienda* where, nevertheless, they must feed themselves, the women may be up much of the night grinding the maize for the *itacates* and *clacloyos* which they will take along. And before a *fiesta* the entire night may be spent in grinding for the festal dishes, not only maize for the *tamales*, but also squash seeds and *pitos.*

With grinding, cooking, occasional sewing, a little caring for the children, and finally marketing, the list of practical activities of the woman is about exhausted. Marketing is done every day. Salt, *chiles*, sugar,

[1] Frederick Starr (*Notes upon the Ethnography of Southern Mexico*, p. 35) says that among the Tlaxcalans a bride before marriage passes through a formal ordeal before the women of the neighborhood. This is called *temaitaliztli*, "trying the hand." She is required to grind and to make *tortillas.*

and spices, as well as candles, alcohol, and kerosene, are rarely bought in quantities; the supply is replenished almost every day. The storekeepers make up little screws of salt and of sugar, to meet the customary demand of purchases worth one or a few *centavos*. Coming to the stores, and especially to the bi-weekly market, the women from all parts of the village meet to enjoy gossip and the satisfying ritual of bargaining for a price. This is a social opportunity confined to the women; a man may make an occasional personal purchase, but never buy the household supplies.

Between the short rhythm of the day and the long rhythm of the year falls the intermediate cycle of the week. Although in places a subdivision of the lunation, this period is everywhere more artificial than the others. In Tepoztlán the week has resulted from an adjustment of the Aztec market days to the European calendar, and from the introduction of the Christian Sabbath. Each of the eighteen Aztec "months" of twenty days was divided into quarters; on every fifth day adult men were required to attend the market (*tianquiztli*). These market days were also celebrated by games and festivals; they were a sort of compulsory holiday. Such regulations merely placed a legal sanction on a system of exchange of goods among the Aztec communities which had grown up to bind hundreds of Indian *pueblos* into economic interdependence.

No doubt the system of alternating market days in the valleys of northern Morelos preserves substantial-

ly the pre-Columbian economic pattern. Only now
the market days fall on days of the European week
rather than on fixed days in the Aztec *tonalamatl*. In
Tepoztlán, markets are held on Wednesday and Sunday. Larger towns have daily markets, with special
days for more important gatherings. In Cuernavaca,
these days are Tuesday, Thursday, and Saturday; in
Cuautla, Friday is an important day; in Yautepec,
one such day is Monday. Thus those who live by
trade can make the rounds of the markets. A vendor
of pottery in Tepoztlán on Wednesday goes regularly
to Cuernavaca on Thursday. There he buys more pottery to sell on Friday in Cuautla. On Saturday he is
back in Cuernavaca, where he buys fruit. On Sunday
or Monday he is in Toluca where he sells his fruit and
buys Toluca pottery. This he offers on Tuesday in
Cuernavaca, and on Wednesday he is again selling
Cuernavaca pottery and what is left of his Toluca
ware in Tepoztlán.

Mexican towns are essentially markets; characteristically the only industry is household industry, and
agriculture usually accomplishes little more than the
support of the community. Everywhere the *plaza*
dominates the town; the only large buildings are
there; it is the center of social life. Even in unimpor-
tant towns like Tepoztlán the two market days break
the week into two periods of lull separated by two
days of special interest and attention. On these
days the Tepoztecans come to the *plaza* to exchange
not only goods but information. Besides the regular

merchants of Tepoztlán and of the satellite villages there come regularly textile sellers from Mexico City and pottery vendors from Cuernavaca, as well as occasional wandering merchants from other and more distant towns.[1] The market day is also a news day.

The importance of Sunday probably varies directly in proportion to the degree to which the individual has taken on city ways. It is not an Indian institution, and in busy season at least *los tontos* do not observe it as a day of rest. But characteristically all classes put on their best clothes on Sunday. When the priest is there the more Catholic may attend mass in the *Templo Mayor*. Sometimes, the "new orchestra" may play in the little bandstand in the *plaza*. Such sophisticated refinements are promoted by the more city-wise minority—*los correctos*.

Like all the simpler peoples, whose food and whose occupations are directly dependent upon seasonal changes, the Tepoztecans are closely attentive to the

[1] There follows a list, not quite complete, of goods sold in the regular bi-weekly markets. Of course the limitation "in season" applies to many of the fruits: (1) Produced in Tepoztlán or the satellite villages: oranges; bananas; *chayotes; manzanillos (tejocotes)*; limes; lemons (rare); avocados; plums; chiri-moyas; mameys; sapotes (four or five kinds); tomatoes; husk tomatoes; sugar cane; *pitos;* acacia pods (*guajes*, N. *guaxi*); peanuts; tamarind beans; coffee; squash seeds; acacia seeds; beans (several kinds); maize; coriander; *manzanillo* jelly; clotted cream; honey; pine kindling; lime; eggs; medicinal herbs. (2) Produced outside the valley: potatoes, onions, and rarely other vegetables, from Cuernavaca; occasional vegetables, as beets, carrots, lettuce, rosemary, small squashes, from Xochimilco, Federal District; pottery from Cuernavaca, from Toluca, and from the state of Puebla; baskets from southern Morelos; leather thongs for sandals and fiber nets (*ayates*) from Cuautla; zarapes and mats, from Toluca and elsewhere; lima beans and such spices as *pimienta*, cloves, and cumin seed, from Mexico City; textiles and notions from Mexico City. Other supplies, and also some that are on these lists, are bought in the stores.

succession of wet and dry seasons.[1] In March, after four months without rain, the fields are burned; the pastures are sere. There has been no work to do in the fields. The dust and the drought, and the inactivity, impose a mood of depression upon the people, which culminates in the taboos of Holy Week. In spring, with the first rains, the hills are suddenly clothed with green and the air is soft and wet. As the face of the town changes, so are men's countenances reanimated. Work begins in the *milpas;* the fruit trees commence to bear again; life is on the rise.

This year-long cadence is broken into minor periods by the occurrence of the many festivals. Benefiting by two traditions characterized by many calendric festivals—the elaborate ceremonial calendar of the Indians and the many saints' days of South European Catholicism—the Mexican folk enjoy a great number of festivals which are in part worship but in greater part play. On probably one-third of all the days of the year somewhere in the valley of Tepoztlán there is going on traditional calendric ritual, although on many of these days it may be no more than the playing of the *chirimía* on the roof of some chapel.

Certain of these festivals, now of course entirely determined by the dates of the Christian calendar, are the most important events of the year to the average Tepoztecan. In the anticipation of and preparation

[1] An attempt is made in the following chapter to give an account of this annual cycle, at once astronomical, economic, and ritual, as well as a matter of public mood.

for these *fiestas*, and in the realization of the anticipated day, the people experience that tension and release, that holding-on and then letting-go, which seems to be everywhere a need of human nature. For many weeks in advance of the carnival it is a chief subject of discussion, and long and elaborate plans are made for it. In the case of the religious festivals, the collection of the necessary money, the building of the fireworks tower, the training of the dancers, the making of the wax candles and the wax-flower decorations, the preparation of the festal dishes—all build up the tension which is to have such pleasurable release.

A distinction is sometimes made between ceremonial occasions which are characterized by restrictions on ordinary conduct and those which are characterized by unusual and pleasurable relaxations from usual restrictions: days of Saturnalia and days of taboo, holidays and holy days. In both cases satisfaction appears to be realized from the alternation of tension and release of tension. From this point of view it may perhaps be said that the calendric festivals of Tepoztlán are, with two exceptions, of the Saturnalia type. In the case of all the festivals celebrating *santos*, the day is on the whole one of pleasure, of wearing good clothes and eating good food, of dancing or watching religious dancing, of drink and of song; and this is even more obvious in the cases of the two most important secular *fiestas*—the carnival and the *Altepe-ilhuitl*. The important taboo days are those im-

ported by the Spanish priests;[1] the last three days of
Lent, when work is not done, water and wood are not
hauled. (Here, as elsewhere, the taboos of the Lenten
period are broken ceremonially by a lesser carnival,
by getting drunk, and—historically characteristic—
by eating meat *tamales*.) The vigils observed during
the nights of All Saints' and All the Dead (October 31
and November 1) are also occasions of repression, of
taboo, rather than of license. The nights are spent in
praying, in calling aloud the names of the departed,
in waiting, in apprehension of the nearness of the
dead—in a repression of the impulses of play.[2] These
are uncanny hours, like the last hours of Lent; and
uncanniness is the very antithesis of Saturnalia.

All the other days of special observation are days of
relaxation, and even the most important commemorative occasions of the church are, in large measure,
play. Although the Tepoztecans customarily refer to
their holidays in two categories—sacred and secular
fiestas—the distinction they make is one between those
holidays which celebrate a *santo* and those which do
not. A great part of the *santo fiestas* is merely fun, and
in the widest sense one of the two principal secular
fiestas has a religious element. The carnival, on the

[1] The Aztecs had taboo days in their *nemontemi*, the five days that rounded
out the calendrical year.

[2] It may be observed that among the lower middle class in Mexican cities—
and elsewhere—the Day of the Dead is celebrated by taking food and drink to
the graveyards and there enjoying a picnic. The final stage in this secularization
and "saturnalization" of this ancient taboo day is to be found in modern Hal-
lowe'en—a children's carnival.

other hand, is the most clearly secular *fiesta*. This is
because it is organized around no symbol of group sentiment. There is practically no commemorative element. Once perhaps there was. The *Huehuenches*, the
masked figures that leap for hours in the *plaza* and
constitute the traditional conduct appropriate for the
occasion, had a meaning,[1] but today they do not. It is
done "for pleasure," and the behavior found pleasurable is of the simplest kind—merely an endless leaping
up and down to a single strain of traditional music.
It is suggestive of the tendency of holy days to become
holidays that it is *los correctos* who manage the carnival, while the more primitive *tontos* have the largest
share in the *fiestas* of the *santos*.

The *Altepe-ilhuitl*[2]—the "day of the pueblo"—is another *fiesta* in which, to the folk, the church is not concerned.[3] It is much like the carnival; there is the same
eating and drinking and buying and selling in the
plaza. But the ancient ritual still observed revives a
symbol of the group and recalls, in a degenerate form,
the ancient glory of the village. A man assuming the
rôle of the semi-mythical leader of the Tepoztecos,
defies the forces of the enemy *pueblos*,[4] and defends
the ancient citadel against attack. This *fiesta* is, indeed, the most truly patriotic holiday of Tepoztlán,

[1] See p. 104.

[2] See the description in the next chapter, p. 116.

[3] Although the ancient pagan festival has been incorporated with a Catholic
holy day.

[4] These are Cuernavaca, Yautepec, Tlayacapan, Huaxtepec, and Tlalmanalco. Is Tlalmanalco extinct? It does not appear on the map.

celebrated far more than any of those in the calendar
of urbanized Mexico. It is the Independence Day of
Tepoztlán, the Independence Day of our own history
at a stage when the Declaration of Independence was
still read before the fireworks.

It is, probably, an old occasion once truly religious,
now in the process of secularization. The *fiestas* of the
santos redefine symbols which are still clearly distinct
gods. But the general state of holidays in Tepoztlán
suggests something intermediate between the condition in a primitive tribe and that in modern city life.
The holidays of Tepoztlán are still individual, unique,
each with its special ritual. For the *fiesta* of Los
Reyes the *castillo* must be made in a certain shape; for
the *fiesta* of Ixcatepec it is traditional for certain
dances to be done. The mere cookery of the festal
occasions is still differentiated and assumes a sacred
character. On Palm Sunday one eats *revoltijo;* on
Easter Sunday one eats meat *tamales;* on the Day of
the Dead several special dishes are prepared; on the
days which celebrate *santos,* and on no others, one
eats *mole verde.*

As urbanization progresses, it may be ventured,
festal cookery becomes less specialized; ice-cream becomes—ice-cream. The holidays lose their special rituals; they tend to become all alike in what is done and
in the meaning they come to have—a generalized
Saturnalia without special symbolism. They become
commercialized; they are consciously reformed. To
this end the holidays of Tepoztlán have not yet ar-

rived. But just to the extent to which the people take account of the coming of city visitors to the carnival, to the *Altepe-ilhuitl*, and modify the celebration in terms of the pocket-books and attitudes of the visitors, to that extent the change is promoted.

On the other hand, the Tepoztecan holidays are no longer like those of a primitive tribe. Under the impact of the Conquest and the substitution of a strange hagiology, the ancient formal religious organization disappeared. Therefore the philosophy of the priests, the specialized explanatory myths which accompanied the rituals, the whole elaborate rationalizing paraphernalia, is gone. What survives is not a ritual system in its exuberant period, but a flattened, generalized system of ceremonial which year by year is slowly becoming more generalized and more secular under the influence of modern city ways.

CHAPTER VI

A TEPOZTECAN BOOK OF DAYS[1]

January 1.—This is the *fiesta* of Santa María de Tepoztlán. At midnight, the first hour of the day before the *fiesta*, the bells are rung in the towers of the Templo Mayor. They ring at intervals, first the large bell and then the small ones, until two o'clock. Then the *chirimitero* climbs to the roof of the church, and in a silence of the bells he begins to play his little wooden flageolet. This is what he plays, or some variation of this theme.

The reedy notes of this instrument, accompanied by a small drum marking this persistent rhythm, rise again and again until dawn. Whenever the *chirimía* is silent, the bells begin again, while the *chirimitero* and his drummer protect themselves against the night air by attending to the bottle they have brought with them. At daybreak they go home.

[1] The present tense is used throughout this chapter as a convenience. No visitor can assert that any ritual or practice always takes place in a certain manner. Strictly speaking, the following account is of festival activity from November to July, 1926–27, observed (except in a few cases) by the writer, and of festal activity for the other months of the year described to him by Tepoztecans. The essential features of these rituals are repeated each year in the same manner. And certainly the form in which this cycle of *fiestas* is here presented does represent the way the people themselves think about them—as changeless repetition.

At noon they are back on the roof of the church, in the shadow of a bell tower, and the *chirimía* is resumed. The bell-ringer is back again too, swinging the clapper by means of a short leather thong. They keep it up until three in the afternoon. Once more, before dawn on the following day, they begin again, and the arrival of the *fiesta* is further announced by the hiss and explosion of rockets.

This is not an important *fiesta*, and except for the inevitable *chirimía*, it is distinguished only by the burning of a *castillo de la noche* in the atrium of the big church. As soon as it is dark, people gather along the walls of the churchyard, and the fuse is ignited. Catherine wheels, rockets, and balls of colored fire, unit by unit it burns, until the last brilliant burst from the top of the tower. Then the *chirimitero*, who has been playing on the roof of the church, comes down and plays standing beside a fire made in a corner of the atrium, while the framework of the *castillo* is removed from its pole. A procession forms, lit by *ocote* torches and led by the seven sections of the *castillo*, carried by seven men, and followed by the *chirimitero* and the drummer and people who may care to come along. The procession goes to some house in the *barrio* of Santa Cruz. The *mayordomías* (stewardships) of the *castillo* and the candles burned in the church for this *fiesta* inhere in the *barrio* of Santa Cruz, and the *mayordomos* are always men of this *barrio*. Arrived at the house of the *mayordomo* of the *castillo*, the framework is put down, there to be kept until next year. A bottle of *aguardiente* is passed around by the *mayordomo*, another fire is built, and the *chirimía* plays there all night.

On the morning of the first of January a new municipal government is elected and installed. But this is accomplished in semi-secrecy by a political clique controlled from Cuernavaca.[1] A group of men crossing the *plaza* after an election, formal only, a number of rockets discharged in honor of the new *presidente*—it all passes almost unnoticed by most of the people who go about their affairs thinking of the *castillo* that evening.

January 2 and 3.—These two days are the occasion of the *cerahpa* and the *castiyohpa* for the *fiesta* just passed. On one of these two days the people must come to pay their pledges for the candles or for the *castillo*, which are paid for by popular subscription. The subscriptions are perennial, made each year in the same amount on the same day with the same ritual, and constitute a promise to the *santo*. For this *fiesta*, which is a *fiesta* of the entire town, people come to pay from all the *barrios*, and even from the little villages around Tepoztlán.

Today there are two *chirimías* playing simultaneously in the houses of the two *mayordomos* in Santa Cruz. The sound of these *chirimías*, and the occasional discharge of rockets and of mortars of gunpowder, serve to remind of their obligation those who have pledged payment. The people come to make this pay-

[1] The year of this study.

ment, and also to enjoy the festal dishes. The *mayor-domo* sits, with his secretary (*escribiente*), at a table in his yard. The secretary has before him a notebook made by the last year's secretary, showing the list of contributors. They are listed by *barrios*, and after each person's name is the Nahuatl name of his house site. At one side of the yard sits the *chirimitero* and his drummer (*cajero*), playing occasionally. A fifth functionary, the *huehuechihque*, waits the arrival of contributors. It is usually a woman who comes. She gives her money to the *huehuechihque*, and waits while he lifts his hat and gabbles a ritual thanks in Nahuatl, the sense of which is that while they cannot adequately thank the contributor, God will do so. Then she passes on into the house and is given *mole verde* and *tamales* and *tepach*. If it is a man who comes, he does not go into the house with the women, but sits down at the table and there receives the festal food.

This procedure is followed in both the *cerahpa* and the *castiyohpa;* both are going on at the same time. The occasion has something of the character of the collection of a tax. Sometimes the contributor cannot remember the amount pledged, and there is a delay while the secretary looks it up in his book.

January 3.—The *castiyohpa* and the *cerahpa* continue all day. The men of Santa Cruz hold a meeting to select new *mayordomos* for the *fiesta* next year. By this time the young men of the *barrio* of Los Reyes have met to clean the chapel and to build the *en-*

ramada in preparation for the *fiesta* of that *barrio*. The atrium and the floor of the church are swept, and the altars decorated with flowers and tissue-paper garlands. The figures of the Three Kings, usually a triplet of *santos* at the altar, are placed so that candles may be burned separately to each. A tissue-paper lantern, in the form of a clock, is hung above the door of the chapel.

January 5.—This is the day before the *fiesta* of Los Reyes. At night the chapel is open and women of the *barrio* come to pray. The men of the *barrio* march to the chapel with the rockets to be set off for the *fiesta,* and then go to the house of the *mayordomo* to enjoy the usual bottle of alcohol. At about ten o'clock *Los Pastores*, the boys who come with staffs of bells to sing traditional songs on Christmas Eve, dance to the chapel of Los Reyes and there dance and sing before the Magi. The women of the *barrio* are up most of the night grinding corn and squash seeds for the *tamales* to be eaten the next day. The *chirimía* plays on the roof of the chapel.

January 6.—On the day of the *fiesta* the *barrio* of Los Reyes entertains friends from other *barrios* and other villages. Everyone puts on his best clothes. In the morning women come to the chapel to burn candles before the *santos* and to pray. After nightfall a small *castillo*, in the form of a bull, is burned in the atrium of the chapel. The *mayordomos* for next year's *fiesta* are chosen at a meeting just outside the chapel.

January 7.—The *chirimía,* now playing at the

houses of the *mayordomos* in Los Reyes, announces the *castiyohpa* and the *cerahpa* for that *fiesta*. In the afternoon the secular entertainment for the *fiesta* is provided by *toros*—a sort of primitive bullfight. Everyone comes to the *corral* next to the chapel of Los Reyes to see the bulls roped and thrown, and to see men ride them bareback.

January 8 and 9.—On these afternoons also there are *toros*. The performance is not varied, but is well attended on each of the three days.

The harvest is over now, even in the fields above the town, which ripen late. The last green squashes have been taken out of the corn. The *milpas* are deserted, except where cattle forage. People are picking coffee and spreading the berries in the sun to dry. In Santa Cruz, where there is much coffee, there is more to do than in other *barrios*. But on the whole there is not much work and there is time to enjoy the many *fiestas* of January. The trees still bear the heavy foliage the rains brought them, but the sky is cloudless, and the outlines of the hills are very clear.

January 11.—This is the day before the *fiesta* of the *barrio* of Santo Domingo. The *chirimía* plays on the roof of the chapel and rockets are discharged.

January 12.—This is the day for the *fiesta* of Santo Domingo. This is not an important *fiesta*, and there is no *castillo*. The *chirimía* plays again and the people of the *barrio* eat the customary *mole verde* and *tamales*. Sometimes the *Apaches* of San Juan come to dance at the chapel.

January 14.—The *fiesta* of the village of Santa Catarina de Zacatepec also falls on January 12, but because it is an important *fiesta* that is attended by people from many villages it is generally postponed until the following Sunday. In such a case candles are also burned before the *santo* on the proper day, which is the "day of the *santo*," while the Sunday on which the celebration is held and the festal dishes eaten is called the "*fiesta* of the *mole*."

Now people are coming to Tepoztlán from Santa Catarina to invite friends to come on Sunday and eat *mole verde* with them. The *cohetero* is building the *castillos*, and the *mayordomos* are superintending the cleaning and decorating of the chapel.

January 16 (about).—On the day of the *fiesta* the roads to Santa Catarina are filled with people traveling on foot. They come from Tepoztlán, Cuernavaca, and Yautepec, and from the little villages of San Juan, San Andres, Santiago, Santo Domingo, Amatlán, and Ixcatepec. Everyone wears his best clothes. It is a very important *fiesta;* there will be two *castillos* and three groups of *Apaches*. The yard of the church is soon filled with waiting people. The devout first enter the chapel to offer prayer or to burn a candle. There are men just outside the churchyard gate digging a hole for the pole of the *castillo*.

Before the morning is old *Los Apaches* come from Jalatlaco in the state of Mexico. Like all religious dancers, they come in fulfilment of a pledge to the *santo;* this vow is annually renewed, and each year on the day of the *fiesta* they come to dance before the *santo*. They march up to the chapel and kneel before the altar. Then they dance and sing inside the chapel. They wear tall, plumed headdresses, embroidered with beads and small mirrors, pink or red blouses, short red skirts with bead and shell pendants, colored stockings, and sandals. Some are women; most are men, who wear long false hair. They dance to mandolins made of armadillo shell. Their leaders carry banners bearing the name of their organization and effigies of *santos*. After they have paid their respects to the *santo* in the church, they come outside and, forming a circle, begin to dance in the atrium. The step is varied from time to time, but the dancers keep their respective places in the circle. Occasionally they sing. The leader sings the verses, and all join in the chorus:

¡Ay! Jesús!
Solo Jesús
Quiso morir en la cruz.

The *cuadrillos* of *Apaches* from San Juan and from Santiago arrive together, accompanied by a band of musicians. They march into the church to kneel before the *santo*, before beginning to dance on the other side of the atrium. The dancing keeps up all morning.

While they are dancing the large candles to be burned before the *santo* are brought in a procession from the house of the *mayordomo* of the candles. Men carry them swung on poles. In front go women carrying baskets of flowers and braziers of burning copal

incense; behind follow musicians. As they come to
the church rockets are discharged.

Then a group of men go to the house of the *mayordomo* of the *castillo* to fetch the *castillo*. This is the
occasion for a social half-hour with a bottle furnished
by the *mayordomo*. The sections of the *castillo* are
brought to the church, also to the sound of rockets,
and bound to the pole. The raising of the pole requires a great deal of heaving and shouting; everyone
comes to watch, and the event furnishes a climax to
the morning. The dancers march off to eat *mole verde*
and *tamales* in the houses of the *mayordomos*, and people disperse to share the festal dinner with friends or
to buy food from vendors.

At about three o'clock the *castillo* is set off. After
dark a *castillo de la noche* is burned. This is the last
event, and most people go home.

January 19.—This is the day before the *fiesta* of the
barrio of San Sebastian. The *chirimía* plays on the
roof of the chapel.

Although there are only sixteen houses in the *barrio*,
the *fiesta* is an important one, and therefore the
"*fiesta* of the *mole*" is commonly postponed until the
following Sunday. Including the *cerahpa* and the
castiyohpa, the *fiesta* may thus last more than a week.

January 20.—This is the day of the *fiesta*. The *chirimía* continues to play. The chapel is open and candles burn before the *santo*.

Saturday, January 23 (about).—In the evening a
castillo de la noche is burned. A load of *pulque* for the

tepach arrives from the *tierra fría*. The women of the *barrio* are up most of the night grinding, for the burden of hospitality is a heavy one, resting on so few households.

Sunday, January 24 (about).—The celebration of the *fiesta* of San Sebastian occurs on this day. People come from other *barrios* and other villages. There are some who come to sell candies and cakes. Women bring candles and flowers to the *santo*. *Los Apaches* of San Juan should come to dance.[1] In the afternoon a *castillo del día* is set off. Everyone in the *barrio* eats *mole verde* and *tamales*.

Monday, January 25 (about).—The *chirimía*, playing in San Sebastian, announces the *castiyohpa* and the *cerahpa* for that *fiesta*. In the afternoon there are *toros*. Los Reyes lends its *corral* and San Miguel its bulls; the same men take part, so that the *toros* of San Sebastian are a repetition of the *toros* of Los Reyes.

Tuesday, January 26 (about).—This is the second day of the *castiyohpa* and the *cerahpa*. In the afternoon a group of men gather at the chapel of San Sebastian. Some are masked with burlap and wear any bizarre rags; some are dressed as women; and some, *los Chinelos*, wear long satin gowns, huge hats, and bearded masks. When all are ready, the "old musicians" begin to play the air traditionally used for "leaping" (*brincar*) and the masked men begin to move toward the plaza, jumping up and down with the high, short, prancing step prescribed by custom.

---

[1] The year of this study they failed to fulfil their obligation.

These are the *Chinelos* who leap at the carnival. Only a few of them leap on this day, but it is customary for some of them to do so on the last day of the *fiesta* of San Sebastian. This event is known as *tlatlalnami-quiliztli* (recollection—of the performance of the obligation to leap). There is no organization of *Chinelos* in San Sebastian, but St. Sebastian is thought of as the recorder of the fulfilment of the obligation to leap. By leaping on his day its performance the previous year is recognized. But to the people today's leaping not only recalls last year's carnival, but gives them a foretaste of the leaping, on a larger scale, soon to be enjoyed at the carnival next month.

Wednesday, January 27 (about).—A great burst of rockets and the playing of the *chirimía* announce the end of the eight-day *fiesta* of San Sebastian.

February 2: La Candelaria (Candlemas).—On this day the little doll (the Christ child), put to bed at many a domestic altar on Christmas Eve, is taken up and dressed. This ceremony is the same as is performed with a real baby forty days after its birth, when it is first taken to hear mass. Today is the *sacamisa* (*tlatlatiyopanquiztia*) of the child God (*el niño Dios; teopiltzintli*). The master of the house where the doll lies in its *crèche* gives a party. He invites his friends, and asks some man to act as godfather to the *niño Dios*, and some woman to act as godmother. The godmother makes clothes for the little image; these may be of silk and embroidered, and quite elaborate. On the day of the *fiesta* at dinner time (about two in the afternoon) she brings the clothes. Candles are lit before the *crèche* and burning copal is set before it. The godfather brings rockets, and often a bottle of wine. The rockets are discharged outside the house while the godmother dresses the image. Everyone is given a drink of wine. The image is placed on a tray and passed around for everyone to kiss. Then follows the dinner traditional for birthdays and *sacamisas:* rice, *mole poblano*, and beans.

February 5.—Today is the anniversary of the signing of the constitution. But this is a national patriotic *fiesta* and of little importance in Tepoztlán. The schoolmaster discharges his obligation toward the school children by parading them with flags and perhaps making to them a patriotic speech. There may be music by some orchestra from the valley in the kiosk in the *plaza*. But most people in Tepoztlán have no notion of what day it is, and observe it not at all.

The dry season is now well advanced. The foliage has lost much of its brilliance, and the silk-cotton trees have shed all their leaves. The paths and streets are thick with dust now, and the pigs gather around the public washing stones where puddles of water may still be found. Occasionally great winds enter the valley and rage around the high-walled basin, clouding the contours of the hills and pulling tiles from off roofs. Then people stay in their houses and shut the doors to protect themselves from the dust.

There is nothing to be done in the *milpas*. The coffee is all picked and dried. There are some who

will buy up their neighbor's coffee and carry it to
Cuernavaca for resale. Many men, having no other
work and no savings, have gone to the sugar *haciendas*
at Oacalco to work there as day laborers.[1] They do
not take their women with them. Sometimes a woman
cooks for them all in the camp at the *hacienda*. Sometimes they come back twice a week to Tepoztlán to
fetch food prepared for them by their wives. Then
twice a week the women spend hours by day and by
night grinding on the *metate* to make them enough
tortillas and *itacates* and *gorditas* to last them three
days at Oacalco.

The entire village has its attention directed toward
the coming carnival—the most important secular
fiesta of the valley. Almost everyone in Tepoztlán has
some share in it, while those who come to Tepoztlán
from other villages come only as guests to enjoy the
hospitality of Tepoztlán. The carnival is the supreme
co-operative effort of the town. In February the men
of San Miguel, La Santísima,[2] and Santo Domingo
are organizing the *comparsas* for the masked dancers.
Musicians must be hired from larger towns, and the
cost of their hire is now apportioned among the members of the *comparsas*. These members, who will leap
as *Chinelos* during the carnival, are busy sewing glass
beads and mirrors on the huge, laterally flattened *som-
breros* which they will wear. Their wives and mothers

[1] This exodus began the second half of December.

[2] The *comparsa* of La Santísima was first organized about three years ago; the
other two groups are ancient.

are sewing them new gowns, or refurbishing the old ones. The members of that family, whose traditional task it is to make the masks worn by the *Chinelos*, are busy cleaning and curling horsehair and fastening it to the wire frames.

Many who will not leap as *Chinelos* are preparing to sell homemade cakes in booths. Others are arranging to bring some pulque down from the plateau, some to go to Cuernavaca for ice to make flavored ices, some to cook *pozole* in great *ollas* in the *plaza*. Some are buying combs and beads and handkerchiefs in Mexico City to sell at the carnival. The carnival is the supreme economic effort of Tepoztlán; it is an opportunity to make money and to spend it.

February 28, March 1 and 2 (about).—The carnival is celebrated during the two week-ends preceding Lent. There are six days of carnival: Saturday, Sunday, and Monday of the first week-end, and the corresponding three days a week later (the *octava*). During these days there are covered booths on two sides of the *plaza* with benches and tables where ices and bottled drinks are sold. In the morning there are cock-fights in the *plaza*.

At just three o'clock in the afternoon a gunpowder mortar is discharged at the house of the president of the *comparsa* where the *Chinelos* are gathered. At this signal the band, which each *comparsa* has hired, begins to play the "leaping" music (the drum accenting very markedly the first of each triplet).

The *Chinelos*[1] leap down to the *plaza*. They leap around and around the *plaza*, occasionally emitting loud whoops. They wear long gowns of satin, blue or pink or yellow, with a square cape hanging from the shoulder. The color and the design of the embroidery vary, but each dancer wears the same long gown with a cape, the same staring mask with recurved black beard of horsehair, the same huge *sombrero*, beaded

and surmounted with an ostrich plume. Each wears gloves and carries a handkerchief filled with confetti.

Hour after hour the leaping continues. The bands take turns playing. At intervals dance music is played and the *Chinelos* dance together in couples. Hundreds of people sit or stand on the edges of the *plaza*, watching the spectacle. When dark comes, the gasoline lamps are lit and each vendor of cakes and drinks along the *plaza* lights a candle. The *Chinelos*, in many cases fortified with alcohol, continue to leap around and around the *plaza*. Men too poor to belong to *com-*

[1] This word is probably from *Chino*, "Chinese", "foreign." When used in speaking Nahuatl it is Mexicanized as *Zinelohque*. The word *Huehuenches* is also used—from the Nahuatl *Huehuetzitzin*, "the old ones" (said with respect). It is said by some in Tepoztlán that the *Chinelos* represent the Pharisees "who denied Christ."

parsas, men from the upper *barrios*, mask themselves in any rags they can obtain, and follow after the *Chinelos*, leaping too.

Later each night a dance is held in the schoolroom, and those men who know how dance with women friends and relatives from Cuernavaca or Mexico City.

March 7, 8, and 9 (about).—These three days form the *octava* of the carnival. They furnish three more afternoons of leaping, of band music, of ices and lemonades and *pozole*. The interest of the passive observers never flags, and each day at three o'clock the *Chinelos* begin again to whoop and leap down to the *plaza*.

March 14, 15, and 16 (about).—The following weekend the carnival is celebrated in Yautepec. Many from Tepoztlán attend, including the *Chinelos* who still have appetite for more hours of *brincando* in their heavy satin garments.

An ebb of interest and energy follows the carnival. The *fiesta* has drained money and strength. Before lie the quite different moods of Holy Week. The dry season is far advanced; dust is thick on the roads; the yards are burned yellow and stiff; the upper pastures on the slopes of the hills glow with low flame and heavy orange smoke night after night where the dry grass has been fired. People keep to themselves, wrapped by a mood of depression and discouragement.

The agricultural cycle has reached its nadir. It is still too early to prepare the *milpas*. A few who have ambition to reduce unbroken ground begin now to clear the brush and weeds from *claculoles*.[1] During this otherwise-idle season men repair houses, walls, roads, fountains. Everywhere around the village householders are carrying stones to replace those fallen from broken walls, or are putting new tiles on roofs. Groups of men, working co-operatively, rebuild broken washing stones, relay stones in the streets, or build new water tanks on street corners.

During this period fairs are held in some of the larger villages in Morelos, and these draw some from Tepoztlán who make the journey usually on foot, occasionally in part by train. The dates of the fairs are given according to the number of Fridays preceding Holy Week. Thus, "the first Friday" is the fair of Chalma and also that of Xiutepec; "the second Friday," that of Tepalzingo. Then follow the fairs of Tlayacapan and Mazatepec. Some men make the rounds of all these fairs.

Palm Sunday, El Domingo de Ramos.—On this day people bring palm, laurel, and cedar to the church to be blessed.

Holy Tuesday,[2] *Martes Santo.*—Men assist the *mayordomos* to decorate the church, to dress the images, and to prepare the candles for Holy Week. A table is laid in the yard of the Templo Mayor, and in

[1] *Tlacololli:* pieces of unbroken land on mountain slopes first reduced to tillage by clearing. They are allotted out of the communal *ejidos*.

[2] Frances Toor (*Mexican Folkways*) says Thursday, but this is probably an error. The old custom was to build a prison for Christ, she says, and imprison the image all night.

the afternoon a dinner is served there to twelve of the older men. This symbolizes the Last Supper. A thirteenth chair is left vacant. The Lenten meal is eaten: fish, rice, and sometimes lentils and the dish known as *revoltijo*.[1]

Wednesday.—Today and Thursday and Friday and on Saturday morning only absolutely necessary work is done. No social entertainment is held, no rocket is discharged. The men do not go to fetch wood from the mountains; the public washing-stones are deserted. The women do only the unavoidable grinding and cooking. People try to have enough water hauled by Tuesday night to last until Saturday. The bells are not rung in the church towers; instead, the *matraca*, a huge wooden rattle, is sounded.

Thursday.—The altars in the church are decorated with laurel and with cedar. On each lie rows of oranges and *toronjos* (the shaddock), with little squares of gold and silver paper pasted on them.[2] An image (El Señor de Santo Entierro) is displayed in a glass-and-gilt coffin. A man sits at the entrance of the church to collect offerings (which are occasional and not made as perpetual pledges) for the crown and clothing of this image. In the afternoon, if the priest is there, he washes the feet of the Disciples. Many

[1] A seasoned stew of shrimps and nopal (cactus).

[2] The laurel and cedar are given away the following Monday. They are used to stop storms, particularly hailstorms. When a storm approaches, people put one of these sacred boughs on the fire and the storm recedes. Frances Toor (*op. cit.*, p. 54) says they are also hung up at doors and windows to keep out evil spirits. The oranges and shaddocks are blessed by the priest and sold; the peel is used for various remedies.

women come to pray and burn candles, and some bring garlands of *flor de chicaltzo* or *cacaloxochitl*[1] to hang on the candles.

Some of the chapels are open, and special images are displayed for veneration. In the chapel of Santa Cruz the *mayordomo* dresses the image known as El Señor de Los Azotes.

Good Friday.[2]—All the ordinary images and the large Christ at the central altar are covered with purple curtains. At one side of the church three special images are exhibited: a Christ lying beneath a purple shroud,[3] a Christ bearing the cross,[4] a Mary dressed in black.[5] All morning people come to pray, to burn candles, and to set incense-burners before these images.[6] A little girl dressed in white with a white crown sits before the recumbent Christ, tending the incense-burner. Among the crowd of kneeling women are four young girls dressed all in black, with their hair dressed in many tight curls, and wearing black crowns. These are the *anxeltin tenapalohuato-nantzin* ("angels who carry the Virgin").

[1] *Plumeria tricolor* Ruiz and Pavon.

[2] Frances Toor says that when the priest is there on Friday morning he performs a ceremony known as the "adoration of the cross." He crawls on his knees between two rows of men to kiss the cross, followed by women and children.

[3] El Señor de Santo Entierro.

[4] Tres Caidos.

[5] La Virgen Dolorosa.

[6] The first two of these images have each their special *mayordomos*. The Virgen Dolorosa is served by four elderly women, the *madres mayolas*. These (and probably also the two *mayordomos*) serve for life. The *madres mayolas* select each year the four *anxeltin*.

In the morning the *mayordomo* of the Santo Entierro comes to the church with the men and boys whom
he has asked to help him. Before the central altar they
build a wooden platform covered with green boughs,
and on it they erect four green trees. This is Calvary.
A cross is laid ready. They also clean the gilt-and-
glass coffin and place it on a litter near the platform.
Then they go to the house of the *mayordomo* for a meal
which includes the Lenten dishes: fish, *guasoncle*,[1]
sage tea, and lentils or lima beans.

At three in the afternoon the rattle sounds from the
roof of the church, which soon fills with people. After
prayers the image of the Santo Entierro is borne to the
front of the church and bound to the cross. Silver
nails are inserted in the hands, and a silver crown of
thorns is placed on the head. The cross is raised on
Calvary. The *anxeltin* carry the figure of the Virgin
up the aisle; it is placed at the foot of the cross. The
tall candles are placed beneath the images; copal is
burned before them. Each woman worshiper kneeling
on the floor lights a candle. Musicians play a dirge.
At about five o'clock in the evening the image is
lowered from the cross and ceremonially washed with
cotton. Then it is placed in the glass-walled coffin and
borne in a procession around the atrium of the church.
The procession moves slowly between two rows of
women carrying lighted candles. While the same music plays in the procession, a man with a small drum
and another with a metal flute stand in one corner of

[1] A flat fried cake of eggs, cheese, tomatoes, and fat.

the atrium and play quite different music—a single minor strain, over and over.

Holy Saturday, Sabado de Gloria.—When the priest is here, he blesses the water and the fire and then holds mass. Three candles are lighted on the water tank in the churchyard; he blesses the water while flowers are thrown into it. A new fire is kindled with flint and steel. People come with coals to kindle and carry home to light incense with. During mass Christ rises; the curtains are pulled down from the altars and the bells ring, not only in the Templo Mayor but also in the chapels. Rockets are discharged. Some eat meat that afternoon; others wait until Sunday.

Easter Sunday, Domingo de Pascua.—Everyone eats meat *tamales* on this day. In the afternoon the *Chinelos* leap once more, and there is *brincando al gusto* (i.e., anyone who wishes joins the leaping). The men drink alcohol again, and many get drunk.

April 28.—This is the day before the *fiesta* of the *barrio* of San Pedro. The *chirimía* plays on the roof of that chapel.

April 29.—This is the day of the *fiesta* of San Pedro. Besides the *chirimía*, the *teponaztli* (pre-Columbian wooden drum), owned by this *barrio*, is played on the roof of the chapel.[1] This is a fairly important *fiesta*. There are generally two religious dances: *Los Moros*, from the village of Santo Domingo, and *Los Danzantes*. *Los Danzantes* appear only at this *fiesta*. The little boys who dance it are drawn from all *barrios*, for

---

[1] On the authority of only one informant.

San Pedro is too small to supply enough, but they are instructed by a *maestro* in San Pedro. They wear embroidered skirts, silk neckerchiefs, and small paper crowns surmounted by a black ostrich-feather plume. They dance around a tall pole and in dancing interweave colored ribbons.[1] They do not sing.

A *castillo del día* is burned; everyone of the *barrio* eats *mole verde* and *tamales*.

April 30 and May 1.—These days form the *castiyohpa* and the *cerahpa* of the *fiesta* just passed.

May 2.—The *chirimía* plays on the chapel of Santa Cruz on this day.

May 3.—This is the day of the *fiesta* of the *barrio* of Santa Cruz. It is not an important *fiesta*. There is a *castillo de la noche* and of course the people of the barrio eat *mole verde* and *tamales*.

This day is also the day on which crosses are raised at street corners, above water tanks, on conspicuous hills. The crosses are hung with flowers and copal is burned before them. It is also the day specially devoted to the masons, who sometimes set off rockets to celebrate.[2]

The first of the rains have come now, occasional and uncertain showers. Only at *Axihtla*, the cleft in the hills where arises the *barranca* of San Jeronimo, does fresh bright green appear, and in parts of the *barrio* of Santo Domingo, better watered than other regions.

[1] This "May Pole" is not necessarily European in origin. Sahagun refers to such a dance.

[2] The *fiesta* of the masons is generally celebrated in Mexico City.

It is still too early to work in the *milpas* in Tepoztlán, but up above, at the village of San Juan, the maize is already being planted. In Tepoztlán, men are hewing beams to make new plows or to repair old ones.

May 7.—The *chirimía* plays on the chapel of San Miguel, for tomorrow is a minor *fiesta* of that *barrio* (the apparition of St. Michael). But little is done to celebrate it, for it is overshadowed by the very important *fiesta* of the village of Ixcatepec, which begins on the same day.

May 8.—This is the first and most important day of the *fiesta* of Ixcatepec. Of all the *fiestas* of *santos*, that of Ixcatepec is probably the most important, although the village is a very small one. For its celebration an organization is formed to include all the *barrios* in the valley. One or two *mayordomos* of these *barrios* and villages undertake to supply the candles to be burned on one of the eight days of the *fiesta*. One of the days is in charge of a village not of the valley. An event of the first day of the *fiesta* is the arrival of the people of this village, Milpa Alta, in the state of Mexico. Every year they come, perhaps a hundred of them, carrying their *santo*.[1] They come to celebrate their *fiesta* with that of Ixcatepec because they regard their *santo* as the same as that of Ixcatepec. They march into the church and place their image on the altar beside the other.

The altar is lit with many candles decorated with

---

[1] But the year of this study, on account of public insecurity and the religious difficulties, they did not come.

paper rosettes, wax flowers, and garlands of *chicaltzo*. People come into the church to light a candle at the altar and to hang a garland on it. Just outside the church under the *enramada* stand two rows of little girls, dressed in white with white crowns and bearing staffs adorned with bells and ribbons. They are *Las Pastoras*, and they strike their staffs on the flags and sing a traditional song of praise to El Señor de Ixcatepec.

In a wide circle at one side of the *enramada*, *Los Apaches* from San Juan and from Santiago dance to their armadillo-shell guitars. At intervals they sing a song to *La Guadalupana*. There is the rattle of a small drum and the high note of a metal flute. *Los Moros* from Santo Domingo enter the churchyard gate. They come doing their little skipping step, to suggest men on horseback. The five Moors, with their helmets, flounced skirts, and black goggles, and the four Christians, in plumed hats and short skirts, weave back and forth in a double row, clashing *machetes* as they come. On the other side of the *enramada* they perform the acted and spoken drama of the struggle between the Moors and the Christians. This takes about five hours. Crowds of people watch them, and other crowds watch *Los Apaches* and *Las Pastoras*.

The sacred entertainment takes place within the churchyard; the secular entertainment is going on outside. There are several ballad-singers, each with his guitar and his attentive audience. Other men are gambling, squatted around the board. There are rows

TEPOZTLAN: THE *PLAZA*

TLAHUILTEPETL, "MOUNTAIN OF LIGHT": LOOKING TOWARD
THE *BARRIO* OF SANTA CRUZ

THE PHYSICAL TYPE

OHUATLAPIL: *HUACALES* AND *BOTES* IN THE FOREGROUND

KITCHEN: SHOWING *TLEQUIL, COMAL, METATE, METLAPIL,*
OLLA DE NIXTAMAL, AND *BATEA*

THE LOOM

THE MARKET

CHAPEL OF SAN SEBASTIAN

SANTA CATARINA: RAISING THE *CASTILLO*

CHINELOS LEAPING

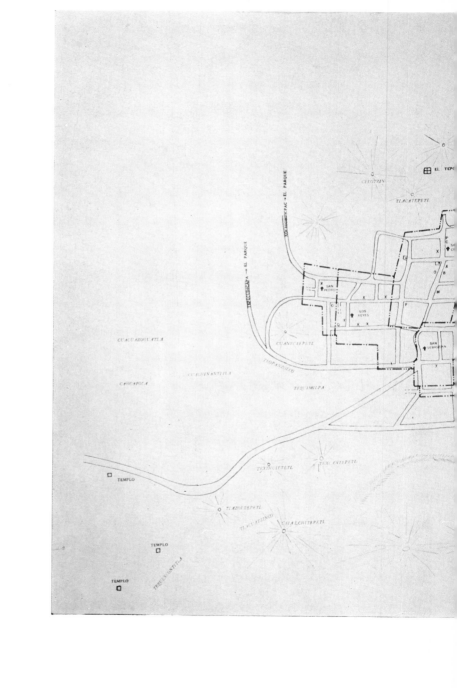

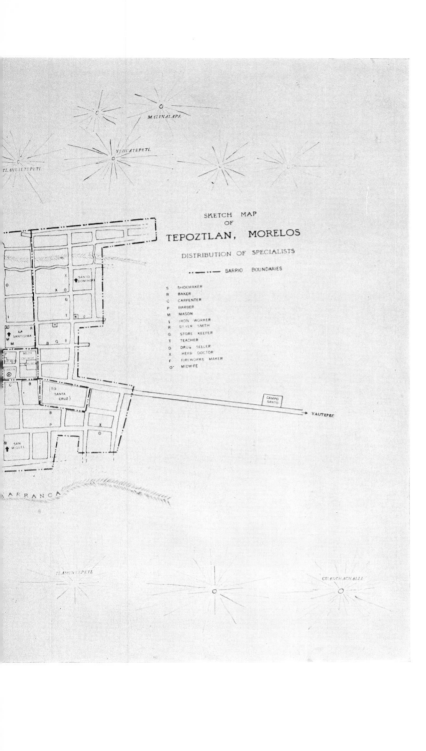

SKETCH MAP
OF
TEPOZTLAN, MORELOS

DISTRIBUTION OF SPECIALISTS

...----- BARRIO BOUNDARIES

S   SHOEMAKER
B   BAKER
C   CARPENTER
P   BARBER
M   MASON
I   IRON WORKER
R   SILVER SMITH
G   STORE KEEPER
T   TEACHER
D   DRUG SELLER
X   HERB DOCTOR
F   FIREWORKS MAKER
O' MIDWIFE

MALINALAPA

YEHUATEPETL

TLAHUILTEPETL

SANTO DOMINGO

LA SANTISIMA

(TO SANTA CRUZ)

SAN MIGUEL

CAMPO SANTO

YAUTEPEC

BARRANCA

TLAMINEPETL

CUAXCHACHALLI

IXCATEPEC: *LOS APACHES*

TEMAZCAL

A HOUSEHOLD

CUATEQUITL: REPAIRING THE PUBLIC WASHING-STONES,
BARRIO OF LA SANTISIMA

CHIRIMITERO AND HIS DRUMMER: AT THE *CASTIYOHPA*, *BARRIO* OF SANTA CRUZ

SANTA CATARINA: LISTENING TO *CORRIDOS*

A DOMESTIC *SANTO*

A ZAPATISTA

A REPRESENTATIVE OF THE OLDER FOLK CULTURE

of booths at which are being sold fruit, cakes, notions, ices, drinks, green corn.[1] People have come from distant *pueblos* to sell the products of their domestic industry—little painted clay toys and whistles. At the gateway to the churchyard one may buy wax candles for the *santo*.

The *chirimía* is playing at the house of the *mayordomo* of the *castillo;* this is set off the evening of the first day.

May 9–15.—The remainder of the week is devoted to secular entertainment: cockfights, horse races, and three days of *toros*.

June 11.—The *chirimía* plays on the chapel of La Santísima and with it plays the *teponaztli* owned by that *barrio*.

June 12.—This is the day of the *fiesta* of La Santísima. It is not an important *fiesta*. The people of the *barrio* eat *mole verde* and *tamales*.

Now the rains have come. Every afternoon the clouds gather over the rim of the valley and the hills are hidden in a low roof of mist. The slopes run with cascades and jets of rain. The air is wet and soft. The ground, long dry and barren, is covered with bright green, and every cranny in the rocks has its unrolling fern.

The rains are brought by the *ahuahque*,[2] "the lords of the rain." They hurl the thunderbolts; the stone beads and spindle whorls one picks up were thrown by

[1] Brought from lower altitudes where it is already ripe.

[2] The *ahuahque* are also referred to as *tlatlatcuapone*, "those who thunder," and as *tlapetani*, "those who cause lightning."

them from the sky. They covet gold; now that the rains have begun and the voices of the *ahuahque* are frequently heard, women who most fear them take off their gold earrings for fear that the *ahuahque* might strike them dead so as to take the jewels.

People are busy now, and contented. There is work for all the men in the *milpas*. The ground is prepared with a wooden plow. For new-broken or very stony earth there are a few steel plowshares. Oxen, less commonly horses or mules, draw the plow. By now the corn is a foot high up at San Juan, but in Tepoztlán a hotter sun demands that the maize be planted after the rains have come. By the middle of June most of the *milpas* are planted. At San Juan the grain is dropped into holes made with a pointed stick. In Tepoztlán it is dribbled along in furrows; afterward the earth is heaped up around the young plant with the *coa*, the flat hoe with a curved blade.

June 15.—The *chirimía* plays on the roof of the Templo Mayor because tomorrow is the *fiesta* of Corpus Christi.

In May or June.—This is the day of the *fiesta* of Corpus Christi, *Jueves de corpos*. Some go to Yautepec or to Cuernavaca to buy little *burros* made of straw bearing crates of fruits and sweets.

July 22.—This is the day of the *fiesta* of the hamlet of Amatlán. (This is the saint day of Mary Magdalene, patron of this village.)

July 25.—This is the day of the *fiesta* of the village of Santiago. *Los Apaches* dance at both these *fiestas*.

August 4.—The *fiesta* of the village of Santo Domingo takes place on this date. *Los Moros* dance before their own *santo*.

August 5.—The *chirimía* plays on the chapel of Santa Cruz.

August 6.—The *chirimía* continues to play in Santa Cruz; it is the *fiesta* of San Salvador, the patron saint of the *barrio*.

September 8 (about).—Today is *Altepe-ilhuitl* ("*fiesta* of the *pueblo*"), commemorative of El Tepozteco, the legendary eponymous king of the Tepoztecos in the days before the Conquest. Men enact the successful defense of the temple on the cliff against the seven attacking towns of the valley. In the late afternoon a tall wooden tower is built in the *plaza*. This represents the *teocalli*. On this climbs a man representing El Tepozteco and others taking the parts of his fighting men. They wear red-and-yellow tunics and feather headdresses. They beat drums and the *teponaztli*. Seven men, riding on seven *burros*, come to attack the *teocalli* and are driven off with arrows. El Tepozteco delivers a traditional defiance in Nahuatl, and the attackers reply with similar set speeches.[1]

September 28.—The *chirimía* plays on the roof of the chapel of San Miguel, and the women of that *barrio* grind corn for the *tamales;* tomorrow is their *fiesta*.

September 29.—This is the day of the *fiesta* of the *barrio* of San Miguel.

[1] See Carleton Beals' article in *Mexican Life*.

October 31.[1]—Tomorrow will be *Todos Santos* ("All Saints"), when are commemorated those who died as children. On November 2 will be remembered those who died as adults. Tomorrow is the "day of the little ones." At eight o'clock in the evening in every home a candle is lighted for each dead child there remembered, and copal incense set burning. The candle is decorated with flowers and ribbons. Before the candles food is set. In the old days this was *itacates*, bean *tamales*, and *mole verde*. Now they offer bread, chocolate, and sometimes chicken or fish. At one side a bowl of milk and little cakes (*mamones*) are set for the very little ones. To keep away the Evil One a jar of holy water is put out, and a paternoster is said while the holy water is sprinkled with a flower taken from the offering.

Every utensil used must be new—baskets, spoons, the *petate*, the incense-burner.

Each dead child is called by name and the food is offered him, while plates and wooden spoons are laid out for each. The family keeps vigil all night.

November 1.—At six in the morning people come to the Templo Mayor and the priest asks a blessing for the child dead. Then all return to their homes and eat the offering of food laid out the night before.

In the evening the offering is laid out for the adult dead. Now the candles lighted are large ones, and instead of bright-colored flowers and ribbons, the can-

[1] This account of the Festival of the Dead is based on the accounts (which coincided) of but two informants.

dles are hung with black ribbons and decorated with flowers of black wax. A large incense-burner is lighted, and it and the candlesticks are black too. At eight o'clock food is laid out for each dead. As it is laid out, one says: *"Ye acitihuitz micailhuitl. Canite inchiaz nomimique"* ("Now comes the Day of the Dead. I will await my departed").[1]

They offer *tamales*, rice, *mamones*, chicken, oranges, lemons, bananas, melons, *mole verde*.

All night people keep awake. They pray, and call out the names of the dead. There are torches alight in the streets. The bells on the chapels strike the hours with double strokes. At four o'clock a group of men from each *barrio* go about asking food for the bell-ringers. People give a *tamal* and a dish of *mole*. At six in the morning the blessing is given, mass is said, and the offering is eaten.

November 7.—This is the *octava* of *los chiquitos*. Again the child dead are commemorated, as they were before, only now no meat and no *tamales* are offered, but only bread, milk, *chayotes*, green corn boiled in *tequezquite*, squash, fruit conserve, and *clascales* made in the shape of stars, birds, dogs.

November 8.—On the *octava* of *los grandes* the offering and the vigil are once more repeated. This time fruit and squash are offered to the dead, and *clascales* colored blue. At noon a procession goes to the cemetery, led by the priest. Music accompanies them.

---

[1] Said in the respectful form (now not generally in use): *"Ye acitihuitz micailhuitl. Canite inmochiliz nomicatzitzihuan."*

Those who have dead to commemorate carry candles. These are lit on the graves. Prayers and responses are said there, and the party remains until eight in the evening. For the responses the priest is given money by all who celebrate their dead.

In December the rains have stopped and the air is very clear. The corn is ripe now, and the harvest begins. The roads are dusty from the feet of men, *burros*, and horses, going to the fields with empty sacks or returning to the village with loads of maize. In the fields groups of men move along the rows, removing the ears from the stalks. A broad needle of wood or iron is suspended from each wrist and used to slit the husks away from the ears. The husks and stalks are left as they were; later groups of women will collect the husks (*totomochtli*) and bind them into bundles to be used to wrap *tamales*. Still later the stalks will be cut down with the *machete* for fodder.

The men always work in groups; the owner of the field has asked them to help him—it is *cuatequitl*[1]— and then when their fields are ripe he will help them harvest. These are social occasions. Each group of men has *la mulita*, "the little mule"—a bottle of alcohol hidden under a pile of corn. The preparation of their dinner is also done co-operatively at the house of the owner of the field, and this is a social occasion for the women. They carry the dinner to the fields for the men. The owner of the field supplies the food and drink. But here the co-operative harvesting ends, for

[1] See p. 146.

the removal of the grain is done separately in each individual house, each member of the family taking a hand.

December 7.—The *chirimía* plays on the Templo Mayor; this, with the ringing of the bells, announces that tomorrow will be the *fiesta* of La Virgen Purísima.

December 8.—This is the day of the *fiesta* of La Virgen Purísima. The *chirimía* plays again. At dawn rockets are set off in the churchyard. This is not an important *fiesta*. There are special masses when the priest is there. In the afternoon mothers bring their little girls, dressed in white as for a confirmation, with white crowns on their hair, to the Templo Mayor. Each child offers a bouquet of flowers to the Virgin.[1]

December 11.—The *chirimía* plays again.

December 12.—This is the day of the *fiesta* of Nuestra Señora de Guadalupe. The usual *chirimía*, bells, and rockets celebrate the *fiesta*. This is not an important *fiesta* in Tepoztlán, although the Virgin of Guadalupe is the patron of the Indians of Mexico. Some from Tepoztlán go to the great celebration at Guadalupe.

The attention of the community is focused on the harvest. Almost every man is working in the fields. The carpenter neglects his bench, the iron worker his forge. The corn factors have arranged counters in the doors of their houses. There they receive the corn as it is brought them, measuring it out in small wooden

---

[1] They do this again in May (the *mes de María*); and in June little boys bring flowers to the *Sagrado Corazón de Jesús*.

scoops, paying perhaps eight or nine *centavos* a *cuartillo*.

By the third week in December the fields below the town are still and empty. The last loads carried by the *burros* are of round green squashes, grown among the corn. Into some fields the cattle are turned to forage. Above the town, where the fields ripen later, the harvesting continues, but the work is on the wane. There is time to rest now, and enjoy the Christmas *fiestas*. Preparations are under way. In many houses, particularly in those nearest the *plaza*, where Spanish influence is strongest and where there may be a little money to spend, the nine *posadas* are celebrated as they are celebrated all over Mexico. By this time the matrons of the neighborhood have arranged in whose house will take place each of the nine *fiestas*. Nine women will take turns as hostess, dividing the responsibility and the expense. Someone has gone to Oacalco for sugar cane, to Yautepec for peanuts. The women are making little paper baskets (*alcartazes*) to hold candies and peanuts.

It is not in one of the larger houses near the *plaza* that boys are learning to sing the songs of *Los Pastores*. In the yard of a smaller, more Indian house in some street off the *plaza* a score or more of boys are seated on the ground learning the songs from a *maestro* who is the repository of this local tradition.

The *mayordomos*, with their assistants, decorate the chapels with flowers and cedar boughs and colored tissue paper. People cut branches of poinsettia, now

very abundant, and bring them to Mexico City for
sale.

December 16.—The first of the *posadas* takes place
on this date. At dusk the flare and boom of rockets
make known the houses where the *fiestas* will be celebrated. Little groups of youths and men drift to the
wall, to laugh and whisper and stare over the wall.
The first part of the *fiesta* is religious, and it is not
good form for men outside the family to take part.
Behind the wall Mary and Joseph seek a lodging for
the night. A candle-lit procession, bearing on a litter
small wax and paper figures of the Holy Family, waits
outside the door. The ritual dialogue is repeated; the
wayfarers, begging admittance, are challenged from
within. It is all done gravely and with feeling; no one
relaxes his serious attention. At last the door opens;
the procession passes into the house. As the candles
pass one by one into the house the yard darkens while
the glow now streams out of the cracks in the door.
The men move closer to the door.

Inside the matron of the house leads the prayers
and responses. The images are placed behind candles,
as at an altar. All the women remain kneeling, repeat-
ing the prayers. Suddenly the prayers cease, to give
way to the gay *piñata* song.

The ritual of worship ends; the ritual of play begins.
The door opens; some of the men go in. The mistress
of the house distributes the *alcartazes*. Everyone is
given a handful of sugar-cane joints, another of *tejocotes*, another of peanuts. The party goes out again

into the yard; there is no procession now; people talk
and laugh. A pottery jar, an *olla*, hung with tissue-
paper streamers, is suspended about seven feet from
the ground. This is the *piñata*. The smallest children,
blindfolded, are first given a chance to break the
piñata with a stick. They are turned about to confuse
their sense of direction. Too good an aim is at first discouraged; a proper climax must be reached. When at
last the jar is broken the children scramble in the dust
for the scattered candies.

December 16–24.—The festal feeling grows during
the nine nights of the *posadas*. The few gasoline street
lamps, purchased by some of the neighborhoods, usually left dark, are burning in the street corners. More
people are in the streets now after nightfall. The fireworks-makers are busy, selling the rockets they have
been making for the *fiestas*. Every evening, in half-a-
dozen places in the village, sheaves of light burst suddenly into the night. Some of the chapels are open;
women come to pray or to light another candle. In
the chapel of La Santísima, and perhaps in that of
Santa Cruz, two *barrios* where Catholic religious ritual
is most likely to be observed, there are *posadas* which
the *mayordomo* of the *santo* has arranged. Then the
procession moves slowly around the churchyard to the
"old music." Mary and Joseph seek a lodging at the
door of the chapel; admitted, the effigies are carried
up to the altar. The prayers are said, and, as elsewhere, when the *piñata* song is sung, men who have
been waiting outside the churchyard come in. The

prayers give way to play; the temple becomes the scene of a party.

December 23.—Pilgrims pass through Tepoztlán on their way to the shrine at Chalma. They carry staffs surmounted by the cross, or baskets of food; some bear flutes and drums. Some sing *alabados* ("chants of praise") as they go. They pause in houses along their road to rest and gossip. At midnight a few from Tepoztlán take the road for Chalma.

December 24.—This is *la Noche Buena*. In the morning women come to the market place to sell *tetzmixochitl*. There are two kinds, red[1] and yellow.[2] This is the only day in the year when these flowers are sold. They are used to prepare the altar at which at midnight the newborn Christ—a small doll—is put to bed. He is the "child God" (*el niño Dios*), "the divine child" (*teopiltzintli*). Girls and women buy these flowers; with these and cedar boughs the shrine is made. At night, after the last *posada*, people do not go to bed. There are lights in many houses; the chapels remain open. At midnight, in some homes and chapels, the Christ child is laid in his cradle behind the candles lit to him. The women kneel and sing the traditional lullaby.[3]

Before midnight people are out in the streets, waiting for *Los Pastores*. The festal feeling has accumulated; everyone is intent on the midnight ceremonies.

[1] *Sedum dendroicum* Moc. and Sessi.

[2] *Sedum sp.*

[3] Printed in *Mexican Folkways*, Vol. II, No. 5 (Dec.–Jan., 1926).

The boys gather at the house of the *maestro* who taught them. From there a sound of singing comes, and the jingling of bells. Up the rocky street appears a light—many lights. Five or six globes of illumination shift and swing against the blackness. Some are stars, some are crescents. The singing grows louder. "Here come the stars of brilliant light, bearing the news that Jesus now is born."

> Vienen las estrellas con brillante luz
> Dando las noticias ya nació Jesús.

Each boy wears a cloth bound over his head and hanging down the back. Each carries a staff of bells, and these staffs beat the measure of the music on the cobbles. The candles within the tissue-paper stars, borne on poles, cast a faint illumination for their feet. Followed by a crowd of people, the globes of light pass slowly across the *plaza*, through the gate of the churchyard up to the door of the church. The church, for a year a place of silence, rings with sudden echoes. The singers move up to the altar, banging their staffs on the flags. The people following drop to their knees. Under the cross *Los Pastores* halt. They continue shouting the song, banging the staffs, until almost dawn.

December 31.—Tomorrow will be the *fiesta of* Santa María de Tepoztlán. The *chirimía* plays on the roof of the Templo Mayor. The *cohetero* is completing the *castillo* to be burned for the *fiesta*.

Some people discharge rockets at midnight to usher in the New Year.

CHAPTER VII

THE RITUAL OF LIFE AND DEATH

The course of the individual life has its times of tension too, and the fact that these moments—periods of pause, of fear, of transition—are nearly always the occasions of special ceremony has frequently been noted. Although it has not been attempted in the present sketch, such crisis rites would seem to present another opportunity to study the process of transition from folk to urban culture. In the simpler societies the rites of passage are an inseparable mixture of practical, magical, and religious elements. The disposition to do something which accompanies the crisis results in behavior which is in part practical and in part merely expressive. When not checked and modified by the pressure of practical needs or by the development of habits of rational thinking, the expressive elements continue along with the practical in one interwoven pattern of tradition. But in modern Western societies the expressive and the practical elements diverge into two quite different contexts. From the former the magical elements tend to fall away; what is done is more rationally comprehended and is year by year modified in accordance with the development of technique. The expressive elements are institutionalized and in part fall under the direction of the church. The technique of the obstetrician is remote from the religious ritual of baptism; the practical problem of disposing of a dead body is attacked by a practical specialist, while the expression of the feelings of the bereaved is assisted by conventionalized ritual which is religious rather than magical.

Such, at least, is the suggestion coming from the literature; it is made also by the materials from Tepoztlán. In this village the practices followed by one family or another on occasions of marriage, death, and most particularly birth, probably differ considerably; and these differences will, it seems clear, be found to depend largely on the degree of sophistication of the family considered. *Los tontos* preserve the old traditional practices; with them the magical and the practical are still an inseparable whole. An informant from this group describes the practice of putting tallow on the umbilical cord of a newborn child and that of burying the placenta underneath the fireplace with no feeling that these customs are of different sorts; because in her group they are no different. Both equally affect welfare; one might just as well be omitted as the other. The midwife is magician-priest rather than obstetrician; she eats the same food as her patient as long as their relation of intimacy is maintained during postnatal care. But among *los correctos* there is probably a tendency to relegate the non-practical usages to the rank of superstitions, and to omit them entirely. This tendency grows, and grows slowly; the society is not breaking down; it is merely changing, and the gradual process of change can be observed, it would seem, in the diffusion of tools and rational techniques from *los correctos* to *los tontos*.

The materials which can be offered here are too scanty to permit even a beginning of such a study. They are indeed inadequate to give a balanced description of all the commoner practices in connection with life-crises. But they may be offered so that the merely depictive aspect of this study may be more nearly complete, and so that the cadence of a Tepoztecan life may be at least outlined.[1]

A pregnant woman keeps largely to the seclusion of her own home. There are no important taboos on women during pregnancy. "If she suddenly wants to eat something, and cannot get it, she takes *tzacxochitl*[2] so that the child will not fall." After three months of pregnancy she goes to the *barranca* to bathe. She may do this many times before the birth.

When the time of delivery comes, she is assisted by a midwife [S. *partera;* N. *amantecatl*]. The midwife cuts the umbilical cord with scissors, measuring four fingers' length from the child. Then the cord is carefully tied with cotton thread which has been doubled or quadrupled and the end of the cord is burned well with a tallow candle in order that it may not bleed. Tallow from the candle is put on the thread, and the child is tied up with a band. In about three days the cord will fall off, but every day until that time fresh tallow is put on. When the cord has fallen, tallow is put on for the last time. The umbilical cord is preserved

---

[1] The materials on birth customs were secured by Margaret Park Redfield. They were nearly all obtained from one informant, a woman of middle age, who had borne nine children. She represents the typical *tonta;* and it is probable that what she described is characteristic of the majority of births in Tepoztlán. Information on marriage customs is much less complete; it was obtained from three informants, two *tontos* and one *correcto.* That on death customs is more complete, and probably the customs here vary little from family to family. The writer attended many funerals.

[2] *Laelium* sp. She takes an infusion of the pseudo-bulb.

for use as a remedy for eye trouble. In correct practice the after-birth is buried in the hearth [*tlequil*]. Ashes are put over it and then the fire is lighted.[1] "Some throw the afterbirth into the *corral* but this is not good because then the mother suffers."

Just before and just after the birth the mother may take an infusion of a plant known as *tlatlantzcametl*.[2] The child is bathed "usually about six hours after birth but always at eleven or twelve in the morning because it is warmer then." Rosemary is boiled with water and put in a washbasin with a small cup of alcohol. As the child is being bathed, still more alcohol is thrown on its head. It is given to wear a shirt of unbleached muslin, a cap or bonnet, and a diaper, and wrapped in a sheet and cotton coverlet. After bathing the child the midwife receives *clemole*, beans, a cup of wine, and a box of cigarettes.

The new mother, who is supposed to stay in bed or at least to remain at home for a month, is cared for during the first week by the midwife, and after that by her own mother. The midwife comes every day and binds up the patient with the *ceñidor*. She makes a doll of rags and ties this against the patient's abdomen. The doll is worn for a month and a half, from the first day on. During the first week the new mother and the midwife, who must eat the same food as her patient, observe food restrictions. For breakfast the mother may not drink coffee, or chocolate, but only warm cinnamon water, which is taken with bread. She may also eat dried meat toasted in the *comal* with a small amount of *chile pasilla*. For dinner some eat nothing but *clemole*, but with washed *chile* and no onion. The patient cannot take food that is very hot or very cold. Milk will chill the stomach. She cannot eat honey, sugar cane, or eggs. During the first two days after the birth the relatives, friends, and neighbors all come to visit. They bring with them pitchers of cinnamon water, or, if it is noonday, jars of *clemole*. After the first three days it is well to give a new mother *necuatole*, which is *atole* of cinnamon made with wild fowl.

---

[1] Sahagun tells us that the umbilical cord of a girl was so disposed of by the Aztecs.

[2] Unidentified.

After the first week has passed all the women and girls of the house bathe together in the *temazcal*. First they eat *clemole*, of which there is a large *olla*. They make little baskets of maguey fiber [S. *estrepaco;* N. *ixtli*] containing pieces of soap for all those who are to bathe in the *temazcal*. If it is the first child, the godmother, who is always present, makes a *cacomixtle* of *estrepaco* with a cake of soap worth ten *centavos* inside it. The new mother is carried to the *temazcal* by a man. The others, including the midwife, bring with them into the *temazcal* a quarter of a liter of alcohol and an egg mixed together in a basin. The body and hair of the new mother are washed by the midwife, and the alcohol and egg mixture is thrown over her. All cover themselves with leaves, and as the fire heats, lie down on a *petate* until the perspiration comes. Then all wash again with warm water, soap, and *estrepaco*. The midwife does everything for the mother, finishing by binding her up with the *ceñidor*.

Every week, as long as she stays in bed, the new mother and all those who are looking after her must bathe in the *temazcal*. Since this period usually lasts a month, this makes four baths. Some, however, reduce it to two weeks—"two *temazcals*."

As soon after the birth as possible [it may even be the same day], the child is taken to the church for baptism.[1] The child is taken by the godfather and godmother. After the baptism chocolate is drunk and *mamon*[2] is eaten.

When the mother first goes out of doors after birth, thirty or forty days thereafter,[3] the child is dressed in new clothes, and the mother, in company with the godparents, takes it to hear

[1] The absence of the priest is most felt in the omission of baptism. "Now our children are like animals."

[2] A cake of egg and cornstarch.

[3] There is an inconsistency in the accounts as to the time. It should probably be forty days, because Christ was presented in the Temple forty days after birth (Candlemas). Gamio, describing the *sacamisa* (not so named there) for Teotihuacan, says that the purpose of the ritual is to solemnize the choice of godparents. Nothing in the Tepoztlán materials would confirm or deny this meaning. But it apparently has, in Tepoztlán, the meaning of a rite of passage; it introduces the child and reintroduces the mother into the community. On that day the rag doll (symbolizing the child in the womb) is taken from its place on the mother's abdomen.

mass. This is the *sacamisa*. This is one of the most important occasions in the life of the child. After the mass, there is a celebration at the home of the child, attended by its relatives; *mole poblano*, reserved for the most important *fiestas*, is served.

There are special dangers and sicknesses to which a newborn child or the mother is particularly liable. The dangers from *el espanto* ["the fright sickness," later described] are greater then. Small children are especially subject to *el daño* ["the evil eye"] and to *los aires* [diseases caused by the evil spirits of the air]. *Ixtlaxolcocoliztli* ["clouds-in-the-eyes-sickness"] is a disease [probably *ophthalmia neontorum*] common to infants. The symptoms are blood and pus coming from the eyes. It is thought to be caused by the presence near the infant of a man or a woman who has recently had sexual intercourse. It may be cured by administering a remedy composed of the umbilical cord of a boy, that of a girl, some raisins, the leaves of *tzitziquilitl*,[1] and the flowers of *sauca*.[2] It is also treated with *Sal de Colima*. This salt is ground and then placed in the form of a cross on the child's tongue with the pestle [*tejolote*] which has first been scrubbed with *estrepaco*. If a nursing child vomits, the mother's breasts are washed with an infusion of *tlamatlantli*.[3] Then the child is allowed to nurse. The mother may take this infusion internally. If a child experiences difficulties during teething, a fly may be caught and boiled with cumin seed. A little of this administered to a baby will make its teeth come out.

If the mother dies, a wet nurse [*nodriza* or *chichina*] is sought. "She earns twenty *pesos* a month and her food." If the family cannot afford a wet nurse, they give sweetened milk flavored with chocolate, cinnamon, or coffee. "But then the child usually dies."

Children are nursed by the mother for two years or more, although milk is early supplemented by adult food. Food given in early life is bread, *tortillas*, milk, beef, bean soup, and macaroni soup. All bananas, except the large, long variety, are considered harmful as causing constipation. Rice is bad for the same

[1] *Bidens leucantha* (L.) Willd.

[2] *Sambucus mexicana* Presl.   [3] *Solanum madrense* Fernald.

reason. Orange juice is bad because it keeps the teeth from coming out. Honey is hard on the stomachs of adults as well as children.

Children may be bathed once a week, but generally at about noon. They are wrapped in blankets like newborn infants and are then rubbed with alcohol "to make them warm."[1]

Children spend their time largely in or near the home, with the other members of the family. There is little organized play among groups of children. Games are few and simple: kites, hobbyhorses, balls. Boys early share in the simple tasks around the house, and girls, when yet very small, are instructed how to make *tortillas* and how to grind maize. Children enter as soon as possible into adult interests and occupations.[2] Confirmation takes place at about eight years.

It is generally recognized that people marry younger in the village of San Andres than in Tepoztlán and in the other hamlets. In San Andres girls marry as young as twelve, and boys when they are fourteen or fifteen. In Tepoztlán they marry at seventeen and nineteen, or later—"a few even as late as thirty." If the husband is already economically independent, he may bring his wife to a house and house site of his own. Very commonly, however, he has not yet secured his patrimony, and the newly married couple live with the bridegroom's parents or surviving par-

---

[1] There is probably occasional, but rare, artificial limitation of families. The principal informant said: "I like to bear children. There are some here who do not—who do not have children. I do not know how that is. But there are *curanderas* who know. They fix them [*descomponen*] with medicine. But that isn't good. God intended to punish us by having children. It is a mortal sin not to have them."

[2] No information was obtained on sex instruction or early sex experience.

ent. "A good wife lives contentedly with her mother-in-law."[1]

The ceremonial accompanying marriage has, in general, a simple Catholic form. Most of the features of the old Aztec customs,[2] such as the consultation of diviners in selecting the bride, the formal exhortation of the bride and bridegroom, the tying together of the clothing of the boy and girl as the sanctifying act, have been displaced by Christian-church ritual. But certain elements remain. The formal presentation of the request for the girl's hand, which must be repeated before formally accepted, was a part of the old Indian custom. The godfather has taken the place of the professional *cihuatlanque*. Minor elements of this custom, such as the bringing of gifts of fruit and food, are likewise survivals.[3]

When the boy has found a girl he wants to marry, he tells his parents. His father and his mother and his godfather and his godmother all go together to the house of the girl to ask her consent. They are received by the girl and her parents. She is not expected to give her answer then. The representatives of the boy ask the girl and her family to think it over, and they come back in a week. They usually go on Sunday. They may come back more than once. If she says "No," the matter is ended. If she says "Yes," then just a week after her consent is obtained the boy's parents and godparents come to her house and put flowers and candles in front of the *santo* in her house. They do

[1] When it was suggested to one informant that the couple might live with the wife's parents, he laughed and said, "Oh, no, there he couldn't even cry out." But a few newly married couples do live in that way.

[2] See, e.g., Clavijero, *Historia antigua de Mexico*, p. 326.

[3] In some villages the old customs are very largely preserved. See, e.g., J. Paredes Colin, art., "Marriage Customs of San Juan Miautitlan" (Puebla).

this on following Sundays too. They may bring chocolate and wine and a *chiquihuite* of bread and put this before the *santo* also. Usually the boy and girl know the matter is settled before the formal consent is given.

The wedding ceremony is performed by the priest in the church, if the priest is there and if the families can afford it. Civil marriage is required by law and obviates difficulties of inheritance; but it is not well regarded and is done reluctantly and with no feeling of a sanction received. Not uncommonly neither ceremony is performed.[1] After the wedding there is a feast, with *mole poblano* ["turkey *mole*"]. This takes place at the house of the groom. His parents and godparents stand the expense. The girl's wedding costume is likewise paid for by the boy's parents and godparents. The relatives and friends of both families come to the wedding feast; sometimes dancing goes on for two nights.

The marriage is in part a recognition of the new relationship between two families: between the parents and godparents of the bride and those of the groom. All these people are now *compadres*, a very close and intimate relationship characteristic of the peasant peoples of Catholic South Europe. The importance of the godfather, who to a certain extent displaces the father in control over and responsibility for the child, is described by Gamio;[2] the relationship is about the same in Tepoztlán.

The family organization is in general European. The details of family relationships among the Aztecs are unknown. But a comparison of present kinship terms in Tepoztlán with those used by the Aztecs[3]

[1] The collected information does not warrant a statement as to the extent of informal unions without any ceremonial recognition.

[2] *La población del valle de Juan Teotihuacan*, II, 243.

[3] This is done in a table in Appendix A.

shows that the old terms are used in so far as they agree with European categories, or are modified in meaning so as to conform with European grouping. The importance of the relationship between parents-in-law is reflected in the use of the Nahuatl word *huexi*, and also of the Spanish equivalent, *consuegros*, to denote this relationship.

The ritual of death includes two conspicuous features. One is the wake, a mildly orgiastic occasion probably more Catholic than Indian. Few pre-Columbian elements survive in the death customs. The paper sandals on the soles of the deceased, the water-gourd and food placed with the body, are probably such feeble survivals.

The other is the sharp distinction between a child's funeral and that of an adult. The former is, as the child is supposed to "become an angel immediately," a theoretically happy occasion, and is accompanied with symbols of rejoicing. An adult is less certain of a place near the Divine Seat, and the funeral symbolism is somber. In Mexico City this distinction is exhibited chiefly in the color of the coffin—white for a child, black for an adult. In some Indian villages the rejoicing on the occasion of the death of a child is more copiously expressed than in Tepoztlán. In Xoxocotla, south of Tepoztlán, in Morelos, rockets are discharged at the funeral of a child, and in some Guerrero villages a dance is held.[1]

---

[1] Not personally verified. The statements in this sentence were made by informants.

When a child dies, the bell is tolled in the chapel of the *barrio* in which it lived. The body is laid out on a table [or bed] and is covered with flowers. Candles burn at the head. A crown of paper flowers is often placed on the head, and a bunch of such flowers in the clasped hands. Food—often merely bread and milk—is placed near the head. The bereaved parents invite their friends to come share their sorrow. Musicians are hired and play all night following the death, while the intimate circle sit close beside the body conversing. The music is gay—the music of march or song. The women remain in or near the house. Outside, with the musicians, remain the less favored men. These drink a great deal; many are quite drunk by morning. There is much laughing, shouting, and quarreling.

Burial usually takes place the next day, most often at about three in the afternoon. All burials take place in the cemetery, which is about a mile east of Tepoztlán. Before the funeral procession starts, the body is clothed in a white-satin shroud. On the bare feet are tied paper sandals, often gilded. A small painted gourd, to symbolize the water-carrier, may be placed with the body. The body is placed in the coffin, but the lid is not put on. The coffin is painted red and gold. The litter is decorated with bright-colored flowers, and these are strewn before the procession as it enters the churchyard. The party consists of the friends and relatives, and the musicians, who continue to play cheerful airs. The mother carries a candle, to be lighted at the grave. When the priest is there, prayers are read in the church. If he is away, the procession passes through the churchyard, up to the door of the church and away, before going to the cemetery. At the grave, if there is no priest, no ritualistic acts are performed. The bodies are placed in crypts; as they crumble away, room is made for others. Refreshments may be taken at the cemetery before the people turn back.

When an adult dies, no flowers are used. The body is clad in black and white. Black paper is used to decorate the bier; the candles burned are black. The coffin is black, and the lid is nailed on before the procession starts. The music played is a dirge. Sometimes the bell in the chapel strikes the hours with double strokes until the funeral. Some families maintain an older custom, when an adult dies, of singing traditional funeral chants [*alabados*] during the night of vigil before interment.

A week after the death of adult or child, food is set out for the soul to come and get before it then sets out for the land of the dead. The eating of this food the following day may be a ceremonial occasion, with friends asked in to share the eating and drinking.

CHAPTER VIII
THE DIVISION OF LABOR

Not only does Tepoztlán maintain itself almost entirely by farming, but nearly every Tepoztecan is a farmer. Most families have at least a small *milpa* in which the men are active during the seasons of sowing and of harvesting. Only the teacher, perhaps, and a few of the artisans and merchants have so specialized their functions as to remain no longer at least in part agriculturalists. Although most of the rural population of Mexico was, until recent agrarian reforms, landless, most of the people of Tepoztlán have for a very long time tilled their own fields.

As with many other communities of peasants or of primitive peoples, therefore, specialization of function has not proceeded so far but that nearly everyone practices the fundamental techniques of maintenance. Agriculture remains as a sort of occupational common denominator. During the harvest season the carpenters leave their benches; some of the merchants close their shops; even the messenger who goes to the railroad for the mail[1] delegates his duties to a boy while he gathers his own harvest, or assists in bringing in the harvest of neighbors.

[1] Daily mail delivery (by carrier) to Tepoztlán was inaugurated in September, 1926. Before that, letters for Tepoztlán were held at El Parque, the nearest railway station.

The municipal government, it has already been suggested, is more formal than actual; and there are few special functionaries in charge of public repairs and improvements. The *ayuntamiento* employs men to care for the building in which the government has its offices, and to sweep and water the central *plaza*. But other repairs and maintenance operations are performed by individuals or groups of neighbors particularly concerned. If a water tank is dirty, it remains so until someone who draws water there is moved to spend the time and labor necessary to clean it. Tasks requiring many men and involving several techniques and kinds of materials are done by men living in the *barrio* where the repair must be made. If the proposed work is considerable, the consent of the *ayuntamiento* must first be obtained. This is, however, almost entirely formal. The local government does not pay for the work out of local funds or employ workmen. For example, when in 1927 a new set of stone troughs for washing clothes was put up where the *barrio* of La Santísima meets that of Santa Cruz, one of the *ayudantes* living in Santa Cruz asked consent of the *presidente*. A few of the elder men of the two *barrios* organized a party to make the repairs. One contributed the lime; another hauled the sand; others labored for a day or more. The *ayuntamiento* contributed nothing but the *aguardiente*.

Such co-operative labor is stereotyped, and bears the special name *cuatequitl*. This word is from the ordinary word for work (*tequitl*) and a root meaning "head," much like the "poll" in our "poll tax." Co-operative repair of streets is *cuatequitl*. The co-opera-tive labor by which harvests are brought in is *cuate-quitl*. So is the co-operative work done in connection with the support of the *santos;* the cleaning of the chapels, and the preparation of the chapel and its yard for a *fiesta*. Such work is regarded as the moral obligation of the individual to perform. The request of an elder to join in such work is not lightly denied. The limited observation upon which these statements are founded would suggest that such requests tend to assume an almost ritualistic character; the request is almost a formula. A group of men go about from house to house, announcing the proposed work. One says, characteristically, *"moztla mitztocaroa cuate-quitl"* ("Tomorrow it falls to you to do *cuatequitl* [of a certain sort]").[1] The word *cuatequitl* is always used.

Cuatequitl is, quite plainly, the survival of com-munal labor reported from both the Aztec and the Maya areas. It is probably characteristic of all parts of Mexico where Indian heritages are strong.

There are, however, a score or more classes of spe-cialists in Tepoztlán, and a description of the extent to which labor is divided is, as always, a description of the intellectual life of the community. A special in-terest to the situation in Tepoztlán is derived from the fact that the specialists there fall into two distinct classes, one of which represents the self-sufficient

[1] In this Nahuatl phrase the Spanish verb *tocar* ("to fall to the turn of," "to pertain to") is used as though it were a Nahuatl root.

primitive community that Tepoztlán once was, and the other of which represents the part of modern urbanized society that it is becoming.

An enumeration of Tepoztecan specialists is not an enumeration of an equal number of individuals; it scarcely need be pointed out that many individuals practice more than one specialty. Some special functions, as those of the musicians, are very occasional. It is noteworthy that in most cases it is a *correcto* who exercises more than one special function.

E. V. was born and brought up in Tepoztlán. His family were by tradition those who made masks for the carnival, and he continues to exercise this function. When a youth he learned the trade of a mason. Later he went to Mexico City. There he learned woodcarving and gilding; these occupations he occasionally practices now that he is back in Tepoztlán. In Mexico City he was for a time a street-car motorman. Now, returned to Tepoztlán, he has a minor position in the municipal government. Occasionally he functions as mason, woodcarver, or gilder, and during the proper season makes masks for the carnival. He also tills his ancestral *milpa*.

L. V. lives in the house where he was born. During the revolution he went to Mexico City and remained there seven years. While there he learned shoemaking. Either there or in Tepoztlán he also learned the mason's trade. Now, back in Tepoztlán, he has a cobbler's shop, occasionally works as a mason, and is also sometimes called upon as a musician. He tills his cornfield also.

The following inventory of specialists is probably not quite complete, either as to the number of occupations represented or as to the number of individuals practicing a given occupation.

Two teachers, a young man and a young woman: Both are natives, of distinctly *correcto* families, and both were educated in the city. Both wear city clothes all the time and have no other specialty but teaching.

The priest should be mentioned, although during the period of investigation there was no priest officiating in Tepoztlán, as there was not elsewhere in Mexico. He was a man of *correcto* family, well educated in the city.

Five storekeepers: These are men of some capital. They have small shops on the *plaza*. On the whole they devote their time to trade. Each makes frequent trips to Mexico City to buy goods. Most become tradespeople on a small scale or minor commercial employees in Mexico City during the revolution; it does not appear that any one of them inherited the business. Besides these five storekeepers there are two young men who flavor and charge water and bottle the result for local sale. These men have considerable communication with the city.

Two corn-factors: These men buy the locally produced surplus maize, arrange for its shipment to Mexico City, and there sell it wholesale.

Three butchers: Their shops are on the *plaza*. The meat is butchered locally.

Two shoemakers: One, a cripple, learned his trade from an earlier shoemaker in Tepoztlán; the other learned it in Mexico City.

Three carpenters: One man has a shop on the *plaza;* the others work in their homes. Tools are simple and few, all of European pattern. These men make furniture, doors, and candlesticks for the churches, also coffins and saddles. Information is lacking as to where each learned his trade.

Four masons: These men lay brick floors, and build walls and water tanks, occasional columns and porticoes on the better houses of *adobe* or stone covered with *mezcla*.[1] The tools are European, except the *coa*,[2] the old agricultural hoe which masons sometimes use to mix *mezcla*. The cost of bringing in cement practically eliminates concrete work. One mason learned his trade in Mexico City, another in Tepoztlán, and a third from a North American railway engineer who employed him as a common laborer to assist in building culverts on the railway near El Parque.

Two ironworkers: These men make *machetes* and incidental ironwork. Information is lacking as to their history.

Six bakers: In the case of two, the trade was learned in a larger city; information is lacking on the others. Each does his baking in a domed *adobe* oven of early Spanish pattern, built in his own houseyard. Wheat flour is imported from the city. Wild yeast is used. The dough is put into the oven on wooden paddles. Many of the special types of bread recognized in the cities are made here too.

Silversmiths: Although these specialists are referred to by this name [*plateros*], and although they do occasional work in silver,[3] they are the odd-job men of Tepoztlán. Each operates a small homemade forge, and is equipped with workbench, vises, punches, soldering implements, etc. They do construction and repair work in metal; repair watches, phonographs, and what little other machinery there is in Tepoztlán. One picked up most of his knowledge while in Mexico City.

Five barbers: This occupation is distinctly an occasional one. The equipment is no more than a razor and shears.

An indeterminable number of musicians. Many men—women rarely—play musical instruments. Sometimes permanent organi-

[1] A mixture of lime and sand.

[2] Already described on p. 50.

[3] Usually silver ritualistic paraphernalia for the church.

zations are formed which assume a public function. A band of
musicians of San Andres are frequently called upon to play at
funerals or weddings. During 1927 "the new orchestra" was organized at Tepoztlán. This was composed of young men, mostly
correctos, who played "modern" pieces, on Sundays or holidays,
to entertain the townspeople. The "old orchestra" is a musical
organization of quite another sort. This is composed of four older
men who know the traditional music used for the *posadas* and for
certain of the religious dances. They play chiefly ritual music,
not current compositions. Funeral music is of an intermediate
type; the "old orchestra" plays at funerals too. The *chirimiteros*
are not regarded as musicians; they will be referred to later.

With the musicians this list grades off into specialties that are so casual, so little differentiated, so easily
taken on and put off, that it is difficult to name the
specialists. Such are the *arrieros*, the men who own
mules or horses and haul goods from the railway to
the town, chiefly for the merchants; the charcoal-
burners and woodcutters; the men who keep and milk
cows and the women who sell the milk; and the women
who sell *camotes*. Anyone may engage in these occupations occasionally; a few devote themselves to
one or another.

There are likewise a considerable number of persons
who stand ready to supply some special need, although the fulfilling of this function plays a very
minor rôle in their lives. One woman keeps *metates*,
bought in some city and held for resale; several keep a
stock of herbs; one of the shoemakers keeps a few
commercial drugs. A casual acquaintance of the town
gives an impression of very little differentiation, but
closer familiarity shows that in any need, even an un-

usual need, there is always someone who is expected to step into a special rôle and exercise a special function for that crisis.

In general, the specialists of the sorts just listed are *correctos*. But there are other specialists that seem to fall into another class, to represent a different type of specialization of function. The specialists of this second class are, in the main, *tontos*. These are:

Thirteen [perhaps more] herb-doctors [S. *curanderas;* N. *tepahtiani*]: With one exception, a man up in Los Reyes, these are women. They have a command of the folk knowledge of medicine. They are called upon in sicknesses of any seriousness. A large part of their technique is the preparation and administering of herbal remedies.[1]

Ten [perhaps more] midwives [S. *partera;* N. *amantecatl*]: These are always women. There is no case in the materials of a midwife who is also an herb-doctor. The specialties are quite distinct.[2] They are called in to attend all births. Their technique has been described in the preceding chapters.

Three *chirimiteros:* These men play the traditional strain of music on the roofs of chapels and in the yards of the *mayordomos* at *fiestas* celebrating *santos*. None of them are young men. The act is entirely ritualistic. There is no pay but food and drink. Most *chirimiteros* carve their own *chirimías* out of *zopilote* wood. This is also a special technique.

Two [or three?] *huehuechihque:* These are men who know the traditional words used in summoning people to pay their contribution for the *santos*, and those used in thanking them when

[1] In asking if a woman sets herself up as an herb-doctor, the phrase is *Sabe hervir?* ("Does she know how to boil?")

[2] There is also some evidence that some *curanderas* specialize in certain diseases.

the contribution is paid. Like the *chirimiteros*, the *huehuechih-que* are called upon only for *fiestas* of *santos*.

Two fireworks-makers [*coheteros*]: These men prepare the *castillos* for the *fiestas* of the *santos*, and make rockets [*cohetes*] which are used for any celebration.

Three maskmakers:[1] These men are brothers. The duty of making masks has always been in their family. Before the carnival these three men devote most of their time to making the traditional masks.

Two magicians [*magicos*]:[2] The existence of these specialists was learned shortly before leaving Tepoztlán; nothing is known about them except the identity of the two individuals. "They say they know how to take a woman out of her house against her will."

These two classes of specialists appear to represent two different types of social organization, and the changing relations between them describe the social evolution of Tepoztlán. Occupations of the first class are invariably carried on in order to earn a livelihood. Those of the second class are to a less extent carried on for remuneration. The *chirimitero*, the *huehue-chique*, the maskmaker, even the midwife and the herb-doctor, perform their functions because theirs are rôles which the group is accustomed to see them take. The specialists of the first class in many instances acquire their specialties adventitiously. In many cases the storekeeper, the mason, or the carpenter has

---

[1] These men happen to be *correctos*.

[2] The *magicos* are quite distinct from witches (*brujas*). The reputation of witches is acquired unwittingly and is not enjoyed. Theirs is not a profession.

learned his trade in Mexico City. Here he has entered into the freer economic competition that characterizes the city, and his abilities have enabled him to survive by means of a trade or profession which he is fitted to carry on. The herb-doctor, the *chirimitero*, the mask-maker, and the others of this group have, it would seem, more often inherited their professions, come into them almost inevitably. This is clear for the *chirimiteros*, *huehuechihque*, and maskmakers; information is lacking as to the herb-doctors and midwives. The techniques employed by the specialists of the first class are those of modern European civilization. Those of the second class are, for the most part, ancient heritages of the Indian culture. The art of the fireworks-maker is a European technique, it is true, but it is one early acquired and incorporated into the folk culture. Information from other Mexican villages[1] suggests that, like other specialties in the second group, it tends to become a mystery, a guarded art transmitted reluctantly to only certain individuals.

In almost every case it is lamented, by *los tontos*, that the specialists of the second group are becoming fewer. There used to be many *chirimiteros;* now there are but three. Young men want to learn to play the violin rather than the *chirimía*. The few remaining *huehuechihque* are overworked. The greater need for

---

[1] "In such wisdom lies precisely the success of the trade and because of its precious formulas, reserved in most rigorous secrecy, pass from father to son as an inestimable legacy, and only on rare occasions to the predilect worker, generally the future son-in-law, as a recompense for great fidelity" (M. O. de Mendizabal, "Powder That Kills and Powder That Amuses," *Mexican Folkways*, III [1927], 15).

midwives and herb-doctors keeps these occupations flourishing, and the art of the fireworks-maker is also a livelihood, like those of the baker and butcher.

It is probable, on the other hand, that the occupations of the first group are increasing in variety. Each new mechanical device requires a new specialist. A few years ago the first steam mill was put up in Tepoztlán; it brought with it the first miller, a foreigner to Tepoztlán. There is talk among *los correctos* of some day putting a small electric power plant in a waterfall near by. This is perhaps remote, but when it happens it will bring other specialties with it. Each of these city-born occupations brings a new world of special interest, a new tradesman or professional who is not hampered by tradition, who thinks in terms of his occupation, who is interested in perfecting it and making it yield more, who continues, therefore, to communicate with the city and take over its changing ways. Such a specialty is not a traditional prerogative, but a commercial opportunity won by competition. The storekeepers of Tepoztlán are becoming its first bankers. The waxing of the first group of specialists and the waning of the second group describes the progressive secularization of labor in Tepóztlán.

CHAPTER IX
MAGIC AND MEDICINE

It is not merely convenient to discuss magic and medicine together; it is almost inevitable. In Tepoztlán, as among other simple peoples, the two fields very largely overlap. Medicine is to a great degree magical, and most current magical practices are also medical. Partly because the rational cure of disease depends on a great body of accumulated knowledge and experimentation, and perhaps partly because the mere expression of a wish to be cured is sometimes effective, magical behavior persists longer in the field of medicine than in almost any other field of human concern. The separation of magic and medicine is, in a sense, a unique event; and even in modern Western society the separation is yet incomplete.

In Tepoztlán the only generally recognized and practiced body of magic has to do with medical cures. Black magic exists in the form of witchcraft; in the present study materials are largely lacking, but it is probably not uncommon. It is, however, surreptitious, and is entering, to the people themselves, into the limbo of superstition. White magic takes in general the form of amulets and talismans,[1] conveying to the wearer the protective power of priest or *santo*. But in the case of the treatment of disease, there is a large

[1] See Gamio, *La población del valle de Teotihuacan*, II, 220. Perhaps older folk amulets, not involving Catholic symbols, are also used in Tepoztlán.

body of public knowledge, of positive practices, which are fixed, traditional, and, in general, magical.

The extent to which manifestations of the morbid are segregated and distinguished as diseases is nowhere very definitely fixed. The number of diseases known is determined simply by the number of names. Any cluster of symptoms may be isolated and given a name; a new disease is thereby created. So the extent to which diseases and treatments are discriminated in Tepoztlán probably varies greatly with the experience and special interests of the individual. It would seem advisable, therefore, to exhaust the medical knowledge of a number of individuals separately, in order to describe the range of medical knowledge in Tepoztlán. In the present preliminary investigation this was not done. The materials come largely from two informants, a *tonta* and a *correcto*. Both described essentially the same symptoms and the same treatments for the more conspicuous diseases. The educated man knew little about herbal remedies, but made more distinctions in medical terminology.[1] The less educated woman showed detailed familiarity with the manifestations and mode of treatment of the diseases designated below as "folk diseases" and a vast acquaintance with herbal medicine.

Of the diseases recognized and treated in Tepoztlán

[1] Fever generally is known as *totonializtli*. Typhoid is *cocolotzintli*, malaria is *atonahuiztli*, pneumonia is *ahcolcocoliztli* ("sickness of the shoulders"). *Ihtecualiztli* is dysentery. *Tzintecopalicihuiztli* is diarrhea with tenesmus. *Yezhuetzi* is hemorrhage. *Necoxonilli* is probably hernia. *Tzompilahuiztli* is catarrh. *Tlatlaziztli* is an ordinary cough; *chichitlatlaziztli* is a hard, racking cough ("a dog's cough").

there are first simple symptoms, such as headache (*tzonteconcualiztli*), earache (*nacazcocoliztli*), toothache (*tlancochcocoliztli*), cough (*tlatlaziztli*), and intestinal disorders generally. These, and the common external disorders, such as tumors, blisters, wounds, burns, insect bites, and fractures, are recognized as coming from a variety of natural causes. Their treatment is specific, usually herbal, and does not involve much ritualistic medicine. For each such ailment there are often many separately recognized treatments, all more or less alike in nature. The notes accumulated on treatment of fever will illustrate.

Alta reina or *tzotzonixtlalli* [*Piqueria trinervia* Cav.] leaves are applied to the soles of the feet.

The leaves of *alta reina* are boiled with those of yerba de San José [N. *sanhuanaxictzi*; *Verbena polystachya* H.B.K.], *malvas* [*Malva parviflora* L.], and the petals of *rosas de Castilla* [*Rosa* sp?], and the resulting infusion is taken internally.

Leaves of borage [*boraja*; *Borago officianalis* L.] are steeped in water and drunk cold.

The entire plant of *tlatlancuaye* [no Spanish name; *Iresene interrupte* Benth.] is ground and steeped with other herbs and placed on the lungs as a poultice. The other ingredients are *rosas de Castilla*, coriander, and a little wine.

The leaves of *espinoncillo* [*Loeselia mexicana* (Larn.) Brand.] are boiled and the infusion taken as a purge.

Leaves of *digerillo* [N. *axaxaxoxihuitl*; the castor-oil bush] are boiled and the infusion drunk.

By far the largest part of medical treatment, especially in the case of these simpler ailments, is herbal. The ancient Mexicans[1] had a wide knowledge of herb-

[1] Francisco Hernandez, *Cuatro libros de la naturaleza.* Also A. Gerste, S.J., *La médecine et la botanique des anciennes Mexicaines.*

al medicine, and a special goddess of herbs; and the Mexican folk of the present day have retained and modified much of this herbal lore.[1] The principal informant on this point collected in the vicinity of Tepoztlán one hundred and ten remedial plants, and for each she gave the name and use.[2]

The infectious diseases acquired from Europeans, which occasionally are epidemic in Tepoztlán, such as smallpox, whooping-cough, and diphtheria, are well known and named. Judging from the materials available here, there is not much specialized folk medicine in connection with them. Venereal disease is plainly distinguished. A common remedy is the root of sarsaparilla, sometimes boiled with tamarind seeds. The only remedy for consumption noted is to boil a piece of china in water and drink it.

But of the diseases which are regarded as entities, and not mere symptoms that may result from varying causes, those most frequently diagnosed and treated are a group which may be termed "folk diseases" as distinguished from concepts of the morbid directly imitated from modern Western civilization. Some of these folk diseases involve supernatural causation, and some do not. The latter class are commonly rough approximations of disease categories recognized in modern city life.

[1] Louis Suc, *Les plantes médicinales du Mexique.*

[2] Those on this list which it was possible to identify botanically are given, with their uses, in Redfield, art., "Remedial Plants of Tepoztlán."

Los biles ["the biles"].—"This is when you cannot feel the pulse. One is very weak and does not want to eat." Various herbal remedies are administered.

El empacho ["the surfeit"; N. *nexuitilli*].—"Children eat too much, milk and tortillas, for instance, and then they do not want to eat." This is apparently indigestion. A herbal cathartic remedy is given.

La disipela [N. *totonqui*, "heats" or *tlachinolli*—a term also applied to the burning of dry grass on the hills].—"A part of the body swells and gets red." There are a whole series of herbal remedies applied as poultices, as well as some internal remedies.

Cuacihuiztli.—[This Nahuatl term is also used in Spanish discourse. It plainly means rheumatism.] "One feels cold and hot; the bones grind together; sometimes a joint has little lumps on it." The remedy is the steam bath in the *temazcal* and the external application of herbal poultices.

Boca podrida [N. *camapalaniliztli*].—Both mean "rotten mouth." "The lips get white and look like pork meat." Certain leaves are toasted and steeped and the lips washed with the infusion.

Costumbre blanco [N. *iztacc-cocoliztli*, "white sickness"].—*Costumbre* is used in the sense of "catamenia." This is a disease of pregnant women. "They turn white and have pain in the abdomen. The trouble may often involve *necaxanilli*, "looseness of the waist" [womb]. Herbal remedies are taken to "fix the placenta."

There are doubtless others. *Tlancuatlatzihuiztli*, "laziness of the knees," has already been mentioned in chapter v, and *ixtlazolcocoliztli* in chapter vii. This latter disease, affecting newborn children, has, it will be remembered, a purely magical etiology.

A small group of folk diseases demands special consideration. *La mohina* and *el espanto* are strong emotional states which are treated as diseases. In both cases uncontrollable passion, or long-persisting moods, which the individual comes to feel are beyond his control, are thought of as morbid entities. The folk practitioner diagnoses them and treats them like any disease.

La mohina ["fretfulness, peevishness"; no Nahuatl term given] is very common. "It is when one has become very angry. One may even get so angry one cannot get over it, but dies. Many things may cause it. For example, one may come to my house, and after he leaves I miss some object I prize. I blame the caller as the thief and get very angry. Or I may break something I am fond of and so get very angry. Children do not get this disease." The remedies are various quieting drinks. Spiced drinks are common, a tea made of lemon leaves, and especially an infusion of turnip peels.

El espanto ["the fright," "the terror"; no Nahuatl term given]. —"One trembles and grows weak and does not wish to eat. Anything frightening may cause it, as, for example, when you wake up suddenly in the night having seen a ghost [*muertito*]." The patient is bathed with laurel that has been blessed by the priest and with orange and shaddock peels which have been placed on the altars during Holy Week.[1]

Diseases thought to be caused by possession by evil spirits, so common in Mediterranean Europe, are apparently absent in Tepoztlán, perhaps because not characteristic of American Indian thought. On the other hand, the idea of the Evil Eye, just as little characteristic of the American aborigines, has been introduced by the Spaniards and is common all over Mexico.[2] The present materials do not contain any reference to the affliction by the name of the Evil

[1] *El espanto* is described from a village in Tehuantepec by Frances Toor in *Mexican Folkways*, No. 7 (1926), p. 31. There the cure consisted of making the sign of the cross, massaging with herbs, and prayers and invocations.

[2] In the state of Mexico, Gamio, *op. cit.*, II, 258; in Tehuantepec, Starr, *Notes on the Ethnography of Southern Mexico*, p. 52; in New Mexico, Espinosa, art., "Notes on New Mexican Folklore," pp. 395 ff.

Eye; it is referred to as *el daño* ("the hurt," "the injury"). There is a Nahuatl term, *oquitzahtzitihque* ("making cry"), and this is the significant symptom.

Children cry and cry, and sigh and sigh, and cannot be comforted. Only children get this disease. It comes after they have been praised in their presence by someone. After the visitor leaves, the child cries and refuses to be comforted. One eye, usually the left, gets very small [*chiquitito*]. The child sighs and complains. Children may die of it. The gall bursts [*quichichicatlapana*] and so they die. Not everyone can cause *el daño*. Only those who have bitter hearts [*yolchichihque*].

The baby is crying today because yesterday you took him to *los toros*, and while he was there some one said, "How pretty! What red cheeks he has!" So now of course he is crying. You should fumigate [*sahumar*] him over leaves of laurel and palm and cedar arranged in the form of a cross in a brazier or a potsherd. Or take twelve *chile* seeds and arrange them in the form of a cross on the *tepalcate*. The child should be held in the smoke first horizontally and then upside down.[1]

If you can find out who caused *el daño*, you must get some *xaltecopalli*.[2] This is gathered on the hills. You can buy it here in the *hierberías*. If a man caused it, make a figure of a man of copal; if a woman, make a figure of a woman. Throw the figure in the fire, and the baby will get well.

The most important single concept of disease is defined not in terms of symptoms, but in terms of causation—of supernatural causation. By far the commonest single explanation of sickness to be given in Tepoztlán is that the afflicted one has been attacked by *los aires* ("the airs," "the winds"). *Los aires*[3] are the evil

[1] This is very reminiscent of an ancient Aztec practice.

[2] "Sand-stone-copal." It has small hard granules in it.

[3] Based on the accounts of four informants, which were supplementary in regard to minor details.

spirits of the air. They are found wherever there is water—at water tanks, in ravines, at public washing-places, in the rain. They are thought of as very little people. The sure diagnostic feature is their appearance in dreams to the person afflicted; he sees them scolding him and striking at him. Then he knows that he has offended them.

Los aires[1] may cause all sorts of mischief. Mere stumbling may be attributed to them. There are certain very characteristic symptoms, however. They disfigure the mouth (*tecamacolohua*); they bring spots (*texiomaca*); they bring pimples or sores (*tezahuama*); they cause palsy (*tecohcototzohua*). Paralysis and scab-like sores are especially attributed to them.

An important part of the treatment for this disease is washing with certain herbs.[2] There are also several internal remedies. Powdered woodpecker's head is one of these. Amulets[3] are worn to keep away the disease. People are careful to keep away from places where water collects. It is dangerous to bathe in the open for this reason.

The washing with herbs should be done at the intersection of two streets. When it is completed, the bundle of herbs is flung away and everyone rushes into the house without looking back. Often the washing with herbs includes fumigation with the smoke of a cigarette.

[1] The name is applied to the beings as well as to the disease.

[2] Esp. *Piqueria trinervia* Cav. and *Salvia microphylla* H.B.K.

[3] Commonly the seeds of *Mucuna*, perforated and equipped with bits of colored yarn.

An essential part of the treatment is the conciliation
of the offended spirits. The Nahuatl name for the disease is *yehyecahuiliztli* ("wind disease"). The word for
"winds" is simply *yehyecame*. But when the spirits
are referred to, they are described with the very respectful suffix *yehyecatzitzin*. The conciliation consists
in leaving gifts to *los aires* at the place where these
spirits became offended, and where, consequently, the
disease was contracted. It is the *curandera* who arranges the gift and takes it to the ravine or washing-
place. The offering must include *tamales*, and often
other food and cigarettes. An apparently invariable
part of the gift is a doll. This is usually locally made,
of bits of cloth. It should have red cheeks. Somewhere about it is tied a bit of colored yarn. "*Los aires*
would not take the gift without this."

I had *los aires* when I was younger. They came because I
went to Axihtla and there I washed my whole body. So *granos*
came all over my body. See, there are still a few here on my
hand. My mother went to an *ancianita* and asked her to cure me.
We paid the *ancianita* four *pesos* and besides we had to pay for
the gifts to *los aires*. She steeped *alta reina* and *mirto*[1] in a bowl.
My father smoked a cigarette and mixed the smoke with the
herbs. Then the *ancianita* washed my body, carefully, with the
herbs. Then the cigarette was taken out of doors and thrown
over the house. The herbs were wrapped in cornhusks and
thrown over the house too. This is always done. Otherwise *los
aires* would come to anyone who might pick up the herbs.

The *ancianita* took the gifts to the water tank at Axihtla and
left them there for *los aires*. She took a doll, two limes, an orange,
three toys of clay, and four cigarettes tied with yarn. After a
while I got well.

[1] The herbs just named.

Sometimes *los aires* demand a chicken [*Piden un pollo*]. Then you take a live chicken and tie it by the water tank or wherever the sickness came, and leave it there until it dies. If you ate it yourself you would die.[1]

Los aires are apparently the extant representatives of some or all of the many specialized deities of disease of the ancient Aztecs. The change they have undergone is that experienced by the European gods that became fairies and goblins. It would seem that the *ahuahque*[2] are also the descendants of pre-Columbian deities;[3] but so far as the present materials go,[4] the

[1] Told by a girl about thirteen years old, a *tonta*.   [2] See p. 121.

[3] It seems probable that *los aires* are in part, at least, the *tlaloques*, the minor gods of rain. The doll is probably the twentieth-century manifestation of the dough images offered in propitiation. "Todos los montes eminentes, especialmente donde se arman nublados para llover, imaginaban que eran dioses y a cada uno de ellos hacían su imagen según la idea que tenían de los tales. Tenían también imaginación de que ciertas enfermedades acometían, hacían voto de hacer fiesta y ofrenda a tal o tal monte de quien estaba mas cerca, o con quien tenía mas devoción. También hacían semejante voto aquellos que se veían en algun peligro de ahogarse en el agua de los rios, o de la mar. Las enfermedades porque hacían dichos votos era la gota de las manos, o de las pies o de cualquiera parte del cuerpo, y también el tullimiento de algun miembro, o de todo el cuerpo; también el embaramiento del pezcuezo, o de otra parte o encogimiento de algun miembro, o el pararse yerto. Estos tales a quienes estas enfermedades acontecían, hacían voto de hacer las imagines de los dioses que se siguen: a saber del dios del aire, de la del agua, y del dios de la lluvia . . . ." (Sahagun, Book I, chap. xxi). Sahagun goes on to tell how the afflicted one asked the priest to prepare and offer the image and describes the ceremony then held.

Probably other ancient gods contribute to the present folk concept. "Estas diosas llamadas Civapipilti eran todas las mugeres que morían del primer parto, a las cuales canonizaban por diosas, según esta escrito en el 6 libro, en el capitulo 28; . . . . estas diosas andan juntas por el aire, y aparecen cuando quieren a los niños y niñas los empecen con enfermedades, como es dandolas mal de perlesía, y entrando en los cuerpos humanos. Decían que andaban en las encrucijadas de los caminos, y por esto les padres y madres vedaban a sus hijos y hijas que en ciertas días del año en que tenían que descendían estas diosas, so saliesen fuera de casa, porque no topasan con ellos, y no les hiciesen algun daño . . . ." (*ibid.*, chap. x).

[4] But see Frances Toor, art., "Cures and Medicine Women," p. 18.

ahuahque are the mountain-dwelling, terrifying gods of thunder and rain, and are not connected with disease.

These limited materials suggest that in general the medical treatments in use in Tepoztlán are like those of all folk communities—a stock of traditional curative acts tending to be ritualistic. But, to a certain extent, there is available to an afflicted invididual the choice of applying remedies of the city. Not a few have lived in the city and have learned to use some of the drugs in official pharmacopeias. One or two individuals in Tepoztlán keep a few commercial drugs on hand for sale. There are drug stores in Cuernavaca, and not infrequently an individual, even a *tonto*, will walk there to secure a medicine. A prolonged toothache, which has survived the ministrations of the herbalist, may cause the sufferer to go to Cuernavaca to have the tooth extracted.

It might be supposed that this choice of remedial systems would in time bring about an experimental attitude on the part of Tepoztecans and favor the extension of rational conduct in the treatment of disease and the corresponding diminution of magical behavior. A collection of cases might show the mechanisms of the process. What affect the city ways are having on the attitude toward disease is, however, probably slowly felt, and so far the traditional cures are paramount. During two or three months of 1925 or 1926 a Bulgarian doctor,[1] one of the few Europeans

---

[1] Known to the Tepoztecans as a German.

to take up residence in Tepoztlán, attempted to develop a practice of medicine in this community of over four thousand. Although well liked, he was unsuccessful in his attempts to secure a practice; people continued to go to the herbalists, and he moved to Yautepec. It seems probable that the city treatments are, at first, simply incorporated into the general body of magical practices. Like people in distress everywhere, a Tepoztecan turns first to the cure with which he is familiar; if it fails, he turns to one less familiar, perhaps a more grossly magical practice from a mental world he has in general left behind him, perhaps an alien practice of the outside world into which he has not yet come.

The baby son of J. S., perhaps the best-educated man in Tepoztlán, a leading *correcto*, fell sick of an intestinal disorder on Monday. On Tuesday J. S. went to the shoemaker to get some medicines from him. The shoemaker prescribed opium and mercury pills and advised that the baby's stomach be rubbed with cold water. This was done. The baby was no better Tuesday, and J. S. sent to Yautepec to ask the doctor there for medicine. Meanwhile the baby grew worse, and J. S. rode up into the hills to find a kind of rose which is frequently steeped to make a remedy for intestinal troubles. This was administered to the baby. At night a patent medicine arrived from the doctor. The following day the baby was no better. On the advice of a neighbor the baby was given more herbal remedies, and its stomach was rubbed with suet. Meanwhile little care was taken with modifying the sick child's food. The next day the doctor came and the child was cured.

R. C. is a man who has spent a short time in Mexico City. He can be described as a *tonto* more sophisticated than most. One spring day he was on his way to San Andres to collect money due him for cattle sold on credit. Becoming tired, he rested beside the crosses at Cuicuitzcatla. He fell asleep, and while sleeping was soaked in a rainstorm. Next day he fell ill, and dreamed that little people were attacking him. He knew that in the rainstorm *los aires*, offended, had attacked him. So he went to a *curandera* in Tepoztlán. She washed him with herbs and directed that he get a live chicken and have *tamales* made to give to *los aires*. She told him that the dolls made in Tepoztlán were not good enough for *los aires* in a case as serious as this, and that he should get a doll from the stores in Mexico City. This he did. But at the last minute the *curandera* stole the doll from the tray which she was taking to Cuicuitzcatla, and *los aires* did not receive it. Someone saw the *curandera* take the doll, and told the patient. He did not get better. He went then to a doctor in Mexico City, who treated him for several weeks, without improvement. In increasing distress R. C. heard of a spiritualist who had come to Yautepec and was curing people through the medium of the spirits. R. C. went to him, but again no cure was effected. He was then urged to try a *curandera* at Santiago who specialized in curing *los aires*. She told him that *los aires* had been enraged by the loss of the doll, and that he must do it all over again. The washing with herbs was repeated, and a new and larger doll obtained. Finally the *curandera* arranged "the last cure" [*la ultima cura*]. R. C. walked to Cuicuitzcatla. On one side of him walked a musician playing a flute to conciliate *los aires*, and on the other side a man with a whip who beat R. C. at intervals to show *los aires* his penitence.

The abandonment of the older, more magical, more ritualistic treatment probably takes place first in the case of the minor disorders. Some traditional remedial acts tend to pass under scrutiny and to be justified because of the rationally comprehended means they employ to achieve the desired result. There is, for example, a notable difference in the way the sweathouse (*temazcal*) is regarded by a young *correcto* on the one hand and an old *tonto* on the other. The former no longer practices all the ritualistic uses of the *temazcal*. There is a growing tendency to use the sweathouse simply in order to get clean, to become refreshed. The *temazcal* is very slowly becoming secularized.

CHAPTER X
LITERACY AND LITERATURE

The latest Mexican census, that of 1921, enumerated 782 adult males living in the *municipio* of Tepoztlán;[1] of these, it was reported, 438 could read and write. Even when allowance is made for the readiness of the census-taker to report an individual as literate on the slightest evidence, it remains probable that about half of the adults of Tepoztlán can to some degree read and write Spanish. Spanish is the only language of the schools; therefore the proportion that can write Nahuatl is certainly much smaller.

Nevertheless, judged by the standard of the modern city, these people are illiterate. And because they are so judged, and because they tend so to judge themselves, they are an illiterate folk, not a preliterate primitive people. Their pre-Columbian ancestors were a preliterate people, for the writing of the Aztecs was no doubt an esoteric art, confined to the priestly class. The first secular school was established in Tepoztlán in the middle of the nineteenth century, but at various periods during the three centuries that preceded that time there were schools of the church. Today two schools are maintained in Tepoztlán, one by the state of Morelos and the other by the federal government.

[1] A total of 3,836 individuals.

The sessions of both are somewhat irregular, but the former gives instruction to a score or more of girls, the latter to several score of children of both sexes. There is also a small federal school in Santiago and another in San Andres. Not a great deal is taught besides reading, writing, and simple arithmetic, and a little Mexican history. Quite a number of *los correctos* have had superior schooling in Cuernavaca or Mexico City.

The mere statistical statement of the extent of literacy, however, is inadequate to describe the advancement of this people. The degree of intellectual development is better told in terms of how much and of what is read rather than by counting those who can read. A truer picture would appear from a study of the uses to which the knowledge of reading and writing is put. Such a study has not been made. This preliminary consideration suggests that even including the minority of the city-wise, the people of Tepoztlán make very little use of the stored experiences of other groups. The best-educated man in Tepoztlán has read much when living in the city, but in Tepoztlán he owns hardly more than half-a-dozen volumes. It is, one would venture, a very unusual occurrence if a single individual in Tepoztlán, except a schoolboy studying his lesson, reads from any sort of book.[1] Magazines rarely appear in Tepoztlán, and in this community of four thousand people no newspaper

[1] The writer himself introduced to Tepoztlán the only technical volume—a handbook of the mason's craft—which he saw in Tepoztlán.

comes regularly. A newspaper costs one-tenth of a daily wage, and when a copy does come to the village there are only a few *correctos* who read it.

Literacy, a technique of communication bestowed by civilization, is not largely used in enabling the Tepoztecos to take over the experience of other groups. With *los tontos*, at least, the exploration of books ends with the brief schooling. But, by those who possess it, a knowledge of reading and writing is much exercised in the everyday affairs of life: in making business entries, in writing letters,[1] in recording the contributions for the *santos*. And, finally, the songs composed in the valley are often reduced to writing.

For there is a local literature. As with all folk peoples there are songs, stories, and legends that are a part of the tradition of this particular community. Among primitive peoples such songs and stories are orally transmitted. They are definitely traditional, and individual composition of entirely new examples is relatively infrequent. Such traditional songs and stories—"folk lore" in the narrowest sense—exist in Tepoztlán. There is a group of tales centering around "El Tepozteco,"[2] the legendary "king" of the people of Tepoztlán. There are stories of animals. Such have been frequently collected in Mexico, and some indeed in Tepoztlán.[3] Whatever aboriginal elements exist in

[1] During 1927 about a dozen letters a day arrived at Tepoztlán, and as many left. About half were business letters.

[2] See p. 26.

[3] Franz Boas, "Notes on Mexican Folklore"; "The Coyote and the Opossum," *Mexican Folkways*.

such tales are overlaid by many European and perhaps African elements.

If the purpose of the present study had been to rescue disappearing elements of a more primitive culture, it would have been indicated to collect materials of this sort. But these older, traditional folk tales do not constitute the songs and stories of meaning and significance to the Tepoztecos. A few people tell these stories, usually to children. This body of folk lore is passing through the nursery to oblivion. It is no longer vital; it does not enter into the important social situations in Tepoztlán.

There are, however, many songs and some stories of local provenience and of local reference which are of great importance in the life of the Tepoztecans. Their character reflects the character of Tepoztecan culture; they are halfway between the songs and tales of a primitive tribe and the tales and songs of a city people. They are only in part traditional; the most important of them are self-conscious compositions, enduring only while fashionable. Only in part do they pass orally from singer to singer; they tend to rely upon writing for circulation and for perpetuation. They are sung by adults for adults;[1] they are the invariable concomitant of all important social occasions in Tepoztlán; and, most important of all, they express the wishes and the ideals of the contemporary people. They constitute the real literature of Tepoztlán.

[1] With the exception of some ritual songs, which are sung by children in public ceremonies.

For these reasons an attempt was made to collect such songs. Because of circumstances to be described it was difficult to obtain the ritual songs; those obtained are no more than a sample. The social songs of ballad type that were collected, on the other hand, probably include nearly all of this sort locally produced and in current favor at the time of the investigation.[1] A collection resulted of twenty-seven songs, including almost two thousand lines.

The songs in this collection easily fall into two very different types, which correspond in general with a distinction between public and private music. The songs of the former group are the traditional chants that accompany some of the religious dances. All local public songs today in Tepoztlán are a part of the ceremonies of the church. They have their prose complement in the *relaciónes*, the texts spoken to accompany *Los Moros*, the religious dance-drama previously described.[2] These ritual songs are entirely anonymous

[1] The writer first began to take down songs as he heard them sung. Later he found that one of the two best-known singers in Tepoztlán knew all the songs in current use. Some he had written down in a copy-book; some he dictated to the writer. At many later social occasions the writer never heard sung a local song which he had not already recorded from the collection of this one leading singer. There is no question as to the local nature of the songs. The ritual songs are used only for certain local ceremonies. The ballad songs that are local are notorious. Not only do they often contain local terms and references, but the music of northern Morelos is apparently of a distinct type. On hearing a few measures a singer will exclaim, "Oh, that is entirely *morelense*." Besides the local songs many songs imported from other parts of Mexico are sung.

[2] The prose text accompanying *Los Moros* was not collected. The many versions throughout Mexico are similar. One is printed in Gamio, *La población del valle de Teotihuacan*, II, 333 ff. *Relaciónes*, some in Spanish and some in Nahuatl, from a *pueblo* in Morelos, are published in Elfego Adan, art., "Las

and probably in most cases ancient. They were probably written by early priests and especially devout natives. They are fixed and permanent. They change little, and new examples do not readily appear. Their tendency is, no doubt, to diminish, as elements of ritual are lost. Often they are in the keeping of only a few, even a single, individual. When the time comes to instruct a group of singers in these songs, such a *maestro* teaches them orally, line by line. There is some reluctance to expose their content casually; they tend to become somewhat esoteric. They are traditional, sacred, ceremonial, public; in meaning they are one with the mass, with religious responses. But they are entirely local, not in type, for the type is widespread, but in specific content.

They are religious hymns of praise of the type generally known as *alabanzas*.[1] The object of adoration is the Christ, Mary, the cross, or a particular *santo*. Some rehearse the episodes involving the birth of Jesus; others describe the Passion. Often the phraseology is taken from Catholic liturgy. But the songs sung by *Los Pastores*, the boys who dance and sing on Christmas Eve and on Twelfth Night, employ a more spontaneous language of naïve poetry. A few stanzas

danzas de Coatetelco," pp. 135–94. The prose text accompanying the ritual of "El Tepozteco," recited on the day Altepe-ilhuitl, is apparently the only traditional public text not connected with the church.

[1] Like the secular ephemeral songs about to be described, local *alabanzas* are sometimes printed on cheap leaflets. A collection of such hymns is described in Mariano Silva y Aceves, art., "La collección folklorico de la biblioteca del Museo Nacional," pp. 269–320. See also Nuñez y Dominguez, art., "The Alabado and Alabanzas," pp. 12–17.

from the song of *Los Pastores* of Santo Domingo will sufficiently indicate the character of this type.

Abran los caminos	Open the roads
Que ahí vienen pastores,	For here come shepherds,
Y vienen sembrando	And they come sowing
Semillas de flores.	Seeds of flowers.
Adiós, María hermosa,	Farewell, Mary beautiful,
La niña mas bella	Most beautiful child
Que nos da esta luz,	Who gives us this light,
Cuadrada la estrella.	Perfect the star.
Corre, borreguito,	Run, little lamb,
Desde la ladera,	From the slope,
Cortame una rosa	Cut me a rose
De la primavera.	Of spring.
Hermosa mañana,	Beautiful morning,
Que lindos colores,	What pretty colors,
Que vientos de flores,	What flowery breezes,
Que plácido olor.	What mild fragrance.
El chivito dijo,	The little goat said,
Ya Jesús nació,	Now Jesus is born,
"Gloria," van diciendo,	"Glory," they are saying,
"Bendito sea Dios."	"Blessed be the Lord."

As with the secular songs, usually two lines are sung twice, and then two more lines, after which the entire quatrain is sung again. To sing in this way all of the four-line stanzas (one hundred and thirty-six in all) of the *alabanzas* addressed to the *santo* of Ixcatepec takes several hours. These verses are sung on May 8, when is celebrated the *fiesta* of that village. The girls (*Las Pastoras*) who sing the song are from Tepoztlán as well as Ixcatepec. There are seven parts to the song. The music, which is traditional and played by *los músicos viejos,* changes for each part.[1] One part is sung outside the church, another on entering, a third at the altar, and other parts are sung when *Las Pastoras* leave the church. On the occasion when this singing was observed an older girl at the head of the double line of girls had a written copy of the song.[2] She gave out two lines, which were sung by all twice; then she gave out two more lines. The song begins:

En tu templo hemos llegado,	Into thy temple have we come,
Padre mío de Ixcatepec,	My Father of Ixcatepec,
Venimos a dar las gracias	We come to give thanks
En tu santuario dichoso.	In thy happy sanctuary.
Christo milagroso,	Miraculous Christ,
Todo de angeles rodeado,	All surrounded by angels,
Gracias te damos, padre mío,	We give thee thanks, my father,
En tu santuario dichoso.	In thy happy sanctuary.

Most of the stanzas are taken up with repeated adoration of the *santo,* and with rehearsing, in phraseology largely taken from the New Testament, the de-

[1] This is not the place to give the musical record (which is only partly complete). But the music accompanying the first part indicates the general character.

[2] From this and another existing written version (the two did not differ much) the text was obtained.

tails of the crucifixion. This narration is interrupted with paeans of praise. The appeal is now to Mary, now to Christ. But it is this particular image that is venerated.

Son milagros que has hecho
   They are miracles which thou hast performed

Porque eres muy poderoso,
   Because thou art very powerful,
Santo Cristo milagroso,
   Holy miraculous Christ,
   El Señor de Ixcatepec.
   The Lord of Ixcatepec.

Pues eres nuestro consuelo,
   Indeed, thou art our guide,
   Señor de Ixcatepec,
   Lord of Ixcatepec,
Y que nos lleves al cielo,
   And may thou bear us to heaven,
   A gozar eternamente.
   To find eternal enjoyment.

Tu has querido este templo
   Thou hast desired this temple
   [Para] adorarte, y dejaste
   That we adore thee, and thou hast left us

La imagen para adorarlo,
   The image to adore it,
   De tu eximia bondad.
   In thy exceeding goodness.

In the closing stanzas a long farewell is taken of the temple and its contents until the next year when *Las Pastoras* will come again to sing. The singers bid separate farewells to the church, the altar, the throne on the altar, the cross, the burial ground within the church walls, the bells in the tower, the hanging lamp. Each detail of the image is separately addressed.

Adiós, rostro ensangretado,
   Farewell, bleeding countenance,
   Ya nos vamos ausentar,
   Now we take our departure,
Adiós, corona de espinas,
   Farewell, crown of thorns,
   Echanos tu bendición.
   Give us thy blessing.

Adiós, manitas divinas,
   Farewell, divine little hands,
   De Jesús tan lastimado,
   Of Jesus, so tormented,
Adiós, llagas del costado,
   Farewell, wounds in the side,
   Abiertas por mi delito.
   Opened by my sin.

Before turning to the group of ephemeral songs, mention should be made of the *mañanitas*. These are songs of serenade, sung by the party of friends and relatives who, at dawn, come to the house of a friend, whose birthday it is, bringing gifts of flowers and food. This custom is general throughout Mexico, and many of the accompanying songs are traditional. They are private ritual songs as contrasted with the songs of public ritual just described; and they are secular rather than sacred. They are of one general type. Reference is made to the coming of morning; the natal day of the person celebrated is hailed; the gifts are announced. The one most commonly used is widely known in Mexico,[1] but there is at least one local *mañanita* in Nahuatl.[2]

The only lullaby encountered in Tepoztlán is the *rorro* song,[3] which is ritually used when the figure of

[1] Words and music are published in *Mexican Folkways*, III, No. 2 (1917), 101. *Mañanitas* of this type are published in Gamio, *op. cit.*, II, 399, and in *Mexican Folkways*, II, No. 2 (1926), 27.

[2] This is as follows:

> *Xi-iza,   tlahtlachia,   yotlanez,*
> Awake,   open thy eyes,   now it is dawn,
> *xihualehua,   xihualehua,   xiczelique   noanimantzin,*
> come,   come,   to receive   my soul,
> *ihuan   noyollo   ihuancente   macxochitl*
> and   my heart   and a   branch of flowers
> *zancualtetzin   timitzhuiquilitz   ipan   nin   huei*
> very pretty   which I bring thee   on   this   great
> *motonal.   Axcan   yenia;   xipaqui,   xihuetzca.*
> day [of thy *santo*].   Now   I go;   be happy,   smile.

[3] This is in general use in Mexico. Words and music are printed in *Mexican Folkways*, II, No. 5 (1926), 42. In a large collection of Peruvian folk songs not a single lullaby was encountered (R. and M. d'Harcourt, *La musique des Incas et ses survivances*, p. 169).

Jesus is put to bed on Christmas Eve, and is also sometimes used by mothers in singing to their children.

In turning from the traditional songs to the ephemeral songs, one passes from the sacred to the secular, from the anonymous contributions to ritual to songs composed and sung by individuals for the sake of pleasure and of art. But, because songs of this type are constantly being made and sung and are then displaced by others, their popularity is determined by the run of current interest and they tend to reflect the interests and experiences of the group. For this reason they are of particular significance.

The ephemeral songs are of the type generally known as *corridos*,[1] a word generally translated "ballads" (lit., "that which is current"). But, at least in Tepoztlán, *corrido* properly designates a particular musical form; the *bola*, the *danza*, are other musical forms accompanying the general ballad type of song.

These songs are sung at almost any secular social gathering. Where guests are gathered to celebrate a birthday, outside the church wall at the *fiesta* of a *santo*, and on any casual occasion when men come socially together, as on street corners at night after work is done, these songs are sung. Everyone knows some of these songs; any man may sing them. But certain men have pre-eminence as singers, and on im-

[1] See K. A. Porter, art., *"Corridos"*; also Dr. Atl, *Las artes populares en Mexico* (Librería "Cultura," 1921), pp. 13 ff., 119–29. *Corridos* are published in *Mexican Folkways*, and many are obtainable on ordinary commercial phonograph records.

portant social occasions it is these men who do the singing; lesser persons would not presume. Women do not sing them publicly, and women are not obviously present at gatherings where they are sung; just as they do not ordinarily eat with men on social occasions.

The songs are usually sung by two men, one of whom plays the accompaniment on a guitar. When the song is ended, little or no approval is indicated. When a number of songs have been sung by one couple, the guitar is offered to some other recognized singer. Such a spontaneous program of music may continue for many hours with no repetition of songs. Some songs have persisted for many years; few last that long. Some that are sung in Tepoztlán have originated in distant parts of Mexico and have become widely popular, but many were composed in northern Morelos. It is these truly local songs which are the subject of the following comment.

Two subjects, everywhere popular, predominate: love and war. The love songs much less directly express the interests of the people, because most of them are highly conventional. The title of such a song is almost invariably the name of a girl to whom the song is addressed. Such songs are supposed to originate as real love songs, composed by a lover and actually sung to his lady. But it would appear, although not conclusively, that in Tepoztlán such an origin is usually fictitious; and certainly these love songs are ordinarily sung by men to men in any social gathering.

They are highly stereotyped, and appear to be merely a conventional art form. The singer ordinarily begins by getting the lady's attention:

Escucha un momento, Porfiria de mi alma,	Harken, a moment, Porfiria of my soul,
Te ruego por compasión,	I beg thee, in compassion,
Para que tu calmes el amor ardiente	Quiet the burning love
Que inflama mi corazón.	That consumes my heart.

Almost always the attitude assumed is one of melancholy, of hopeless desire.

Que triste es quererte tanto,	How sad to love thee so
Y a no volverse [a] amar,	And not to love each other again,
Que después de amores, llanto,	That after love, tears,
Sumergido a padecer.	Drowned in suffering.

En el panteón del olvido	In the graveyard of forgetfulness
Dale sepulcro a mi querer,	Give burial to my longing,
Y negar que te he querido	And to deny that I have loved you
Te lo pido, por favor.	I ask thee, as a favor.

The body of such songs as these is largely taken up with praises of the lady's charms. This praise is as conventional as it is extravagant. She is lovelier than the angels. Adam would have left Eden if he had glimpsed her. The lover would build a throne so he might place her on it and before her prostrate himself. The ornamental figures are elements taken from familiar sacred literature—angels, cherubs, Paradise— and a few names from the classics, such as Diana and Venus. The similes in a more sophisticated society would be *clichés*. Her lips are always like rubies; her brow is almost regularly compared to the rising sun. A well-liked stanza praising Porfiria in such terms appears again almost unchanged in a different song addressed to Concha.

Esos tus chinitos que adornan tu frente	Those curls of thine which adorn thy brow
Me roban el pensamiento,	Rob me of thought,
Parece que miro el sol del oriente	It seems that I behold the rising sun
Cada vez que los contemplo.	Each time that I look upon them.

These love songs are expressive only in that they reflect the degree of sophistication of the group. The form and the poetic mood are not indigenous, are not a growth of the soil; they are borrowed. They have become a conventional art form in Tepoztlán. They are the more naïve forerunners of the sentimental song of city civilization.

From this form only three or four love songs in the present collection depart. One describes the competition of a rich man and a poet for the hand of a lady. In another the lover tells his lady that in loving her he is forced to break the Ten Commandments. Only one love song in the group is told not in the stilted language of a formal poetry but in the true vernacular. It is a dialogue between a man of the people and a girl of the people. They are both, it is clear, *tontos*. He woos her not with the artificial flowers of a borrowed metaphor but with the promises and in the terms of Tepoztlán. Nahuatl phrases are used.

Yo vide[1] un naturalito	I saw a "child of nature"
Que a su indita la paró	Who stopped his Indian love
En un lugar tan solito,	In a place quite solitary,
Que de amores le trató.	Which was just right for love.
Observé las palabritas	I noticed the little words
Que la decía, no sé que,	Which he said to her, I don't know what,
"*Xinechmaca* tu boquita	"Give me your mouth
Para que yo besaré."	That I may kiss you."
Y le respondió la indita:	And the little Indian answered him:
"*Amo, amo*, Juan Jusé."	"No, no, Juan José."

There are eight stanzas. He begs her to yield.

"Selo compraré en seguida	"I will buy you right away
Tus zapatos con tacón,	Your shoes with heels,
Tus 'naguas con brillantina,	Your skirts with spangles,
Que parescas de sazón,	That you may look just right,
Tus arillos, tu mascada,	Your earrings, your silk handkerchief,
Con tu tapalo café,	With your brown shawl,
Si lo admites, prenda amada,	If you will accept it, sweetheart,
Todo telo compraré."	I will buy it all for you."
La indita tiró una risada,	The little Indian laughed,
"¡Qué chistoso es Juan Jusé!"	"How funny is Juan José!"

She remains coy until he makes an improper advance, which draws from her invective, partly Spanish, partly Nahuatl.

"Mientras ti lo daré un real	"Meanwhile I will give you a *real*
Con tal tu amor me lo des,	On condition that you give me your love,
'Hora que hay este lugar	Now that there is this chance
De estar junto con ti."'	That I may possess you."
"*Amo, amo*, Juan José,	"No, no, Juan José,
Zantiquitas,[2] picarón,	Now you see, you rogue,
Bonito quieres hacer?	You want to do the right thing?
Diablo, *nantzin*, barrigón!	Devil, old woman, pot-belly,
Tu no tratas de buena fé,	You don't act in good faith,
Tratas de mala intención."	You act with bad intent."

[1] Vulgar for *vi*.   [2] For *axcan tiquitaz*.

There is a small group of songs written in the same stilted phraseology as the love songs addressed to the lady hopelessly loved, but with a different subject matter. These are songs addressed by singers to other singers. All these local ephemeral songs are written by men in or near the valley of Tepoztlán, and most of them by two or three men who enjoy reputations in northern Morelos as great poets.[1] One poet addresses a contemporary, or one recently dead, in a song of praise. In such songs the similes are again conventional: the guitar is referred to as a "lyre"; the composers are "nightingales." But these songs name the men recognized as *gran poetas* in the little world of these songs, and the intellectual self-sufficiency of the small community is unmistakable.

Por todo el ámbito, Oacalco a Yautepec,[2]
Es una gloria sus cantos al escuchar,
Muy entusiastas las ninfas con placer,
Brindando aplausas a Guadalupe Beltran.[3]

Throughout all the circuit, Oacalco to Yautepec,
It is glorious to listen to your songs,
The nymphs, enthusiastic with pleasure,
Offering applause to Guadalupe Beltran.

However conventional the language of songs of this type, they are of significance in describing the life of Tepoztlán, because they do embody actual memories that the people hold dear and they do enshrine local heroes. It is because the songs of war do just this that

[1] A singer generally composes the words, then tries them on his instrument and puts the music to them.

[2] A distance of about eight miles. Yautepec is fourteen miles from Tepoztlán.

[3] The singer honored.

they are the most significant of all the songs. They
are the songs that record and perpetuate events (*corridos*, in the sense in which that term is used generally
in Mexico). In the cities of Mexico such songs report
dramatic crimes or accidents as well as the events of
war. This class of songs constitutes a sort of newspaper of the folk. Such songs from other communities come to Tepoztlán and are sung there along with
the local *corridos*. But, in Tepoztlán, crime almost
does not occur, and great accidents are rare; so the
subject matter involves almost entirely the episodes
and the heroes of the last great revolution. Dramatic
incidents that happened near Tepoztlán, the local revolutionary leaders, the moods of pride and sorrow of
revolutionary days, were made into music by Zapatista soldiers around their campfires; and now these
memories of which the group is proud are revived and
the values therein are redefined in the singing of the
songs today. These songs are the real history-books
of Tepoztlán, the cherry tree of their George Washington, and their Paul Revere's ride.

These ballads of revolution may conveniently be
regarded as of three principal types: the soldier song,
the political lampoon, and the narrative of a military
exploit.

In the soldier song the Zapatista sings his life.
There are no episodes, no personalities. The life of
the *guerrilla* in the mountains itself speaks.

Soy rebelde del Estado de Morelos,
  Y que proclamo las promesas
de San Luis,[1]
Soy rebelde y lucharé contra el
gobierno,
  Porque al fin nada llegada a
complir.
Con mi guincher, mi caballo y
tres canañas,
  Y descubro la virgen de Tepey-
ac,[2]
Así que haré que respete el Plan
de Ayala,[3]
  O que sucumba cual valiente
liberal.
Mi boluarte los montanes, y no
lo niego,
  Y mi nombre Zapatista lo ha
de ser,
Ante un grupo de Carranclanes
no me arredro,
  Siempre que tenga mi treinta-
treinta he de prender.
Pero al fin si mi suerte no es ad-
versa,
  O sucumba en el campo por
desgracia,
Moriré proclamando con firme-
za,—
  ¡Vivan las fuerzas del sur!
  ¡Viva Zapata!⁴

I'm a rebel of the state of Morelos,

And I proclaim the promises of
San Luis,
I'm a rebel and I'll fight against
the government,
Because in the end it has not ful-
filled anything.
With my Winchester, my horse
and three cartridge belts,
And I display the Virgin of Te-
peyac,
So I will make respected the Plan
of Ayala,
Or I perish as a valiant liberal.

My bulwark is the mountains, and
I don't deny it,
And my name Zapatista, it will
ever be,
Before a group of Carranzistas I
don't draw back,
If always I have my thirty-thirty
right at hand.
But whether in the end my lot is
lucky,
Or I die on the field by mischance,
I shall die steadfastly proclaim-
ing,—
Long live the forces of the south!
Long live Zapata!

[1] The title of Madero's call for revolution (1910).

[2] The Virgin of Guadalupe.

[3] The title of Zapata's call for revolution (1911).

[4] The melody of the song just given will serve to illustrate the type of music
of the secular song. [See music at foot of next page.]

Another soldier song tells of the *guachas*—the camp-followers of the revolution. The mood is one of bitterness and scorn against those false women of Morelos who have given themselves to the Carranzistas instead of to the followers of Zapata.

Siendo contrarias a nuestra causa,	Although they are enemies of our cause,
Los federales en la ocasión	The federals on this occasion
Las de mi tierra sean vuelto guachas,	The women of my land[1] have turned *guachas,*
Hasta suspiran por un pelón,[2]	And they even sigh for a trooper,
Como ellos tienen bastante plata,	As those fellows have plenty of coin,
Y a buen precio les dan su amor;	So they get a good price for their love;
También ya dicen, "¡Muera Zapata!	Now they say too, "Down with Zapata!
¡Viva el gobierno que es lo mejor!"	Hurrah for the government which is the best!"

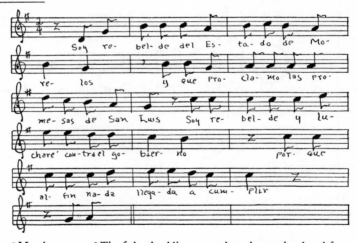

Soy re-bel-de del Es-ta-do de Mo-re-los y que pro-cla-mo las pro-me-sas de San Luis Soy re-bel-de y lu-chare' con-tra el go-bier-no por-que al-fin na-da llega-da a cum-plir

[1] Morelos.   [2] The federal soldiers were close shaven head and face.

Of the eighty lines only eight more need be quoted here:

Y si me niegan esas caricias	And if they deny me those caresses of theirs
Porque mi traje no es de rural,	Because my costume isn't that of a federal,
Pueden borrarme de su lista	They can scratch me off their list
Que por sentido no me he de dar.	And I will not take offense at that.
Mejor prefiero ser Zapatista	I'd rather be a Zapatista
Y no verdugo, cruel federal,	And not a beastly, cruel federal,
Que hombres sensibles la vida quitan	Let sensible men quit life
Cuando les llegan a derrotar.	When those fellows succeed in routing them.

The type of political lampoon is illustrated by the "Corrido de Don Venustiano." In this, Carranza, the protagonist of Zapata, is mockingly addressed by the singing Zapatista.

El señor don Venustiano quería ser respetado	Mr. Don Venustiano wanted to be respected
Como un gran veterano de nuestra libertad,	As a great fighter for our liberty,
Pero este pobre pueblo que se halla enfurecido	But this poor people that is enraged
Maldice a cada hora su barbara ansiedad	Every hour curses his barbarous eagerness.
¿De que le sirve a Usted, señor don Venustiano,	Since when there were at your service, Mr. Don Venustiano,
La ciencia de su frente y la edad que tiene Usted?	The wisdom of your forehead and the great age which is yours?
Si todos sus asuntos marchan por mal camino,	If all your affairs go by such a bad road,
No tiene Usted principios de ser libertador.	You haven't the principles to be a liberator.
Pues ya se puede huir a la vieja Europa	Well, now you can flee to old Europe
Usted y toda su tropa que vino a conquistar,	Yourself, and all your troop that came to conquer,

Porque todo fué un sueño, el triunfo que le tocó,	Because it was all a dream, that triumph of yours,
Por eso le sofoca la gran revolución.	That is why the great revolution smothered you.
¿ Pues que pensaba Usted, Señor don Venustiano,	Well, what did you think, Mr. Venustiano,
Que con su gran esfuerzo vencería la nación?	That with your great force you would conquer the nation?
Pues sepa Usted y entienda que el pueblo Mexicano	Well, know and learn that the Mexican people
Despoja los tiranos de nuestra libertad.	Cuts down the tyrants of our liberty.

War in Mexico is also politics, and it is waged in terms of personalities, of heroes, and of tyrants. The military songs of the narrative type usually recount some heroic act of one or another local leader. Of these the greatest is Emiliano Zapata, but other lesser men are also sung. Characteristically it is the tragic death, accomplished through perfidious betrayal, that is the subject of the ballad. The captured general defies his captors, makes a patriotic speech, and is shot. Ballads of this type are specific as to names and dates —they are intermediate in character between, and identical in function with, the legends of a tribal people and the history-books of primary education in city life. "On the thirtieth of May," begins the "Ballad of Serna," "in Santana Clacotenco[1] was Don Sirino Serna, with his faithful brigade, guarding the *plaza*, when he found himself taken by surprise." A traitor named Quintero, an "Iscariot," betrayed him. "It was a little after four o'clock on that sad morning

---

[1] Not far north of Tepoztlán, in the Federal District.

when the cavalry surrounded him." There was a short but bitter struggle; Serna was taken by Quintero and stood up to be shot. His dying words are given:

"No crea Usted, Quintero, que con amenazas,
    Tal vez yo cambie de resolución,
Soy su prisionero, y ¡Que viva Zapata!
    ¡Mueran los traidores de nuestra nación!
En aquel momento cayó aquel valiente,
    Bañado en su sangre por un projectil,
Don Sirino Serna nos dijo, "Fijense,
    Nos dejó un ejemplo digno de valor civil."

"Don't think, Quintero, that because of threats,
    Perhaps my resolution wavers,
I am your prisoner, and long live Zapata!
Die the traitors of our country!
At that moment that brave man fell,
Bathed in his blood by a bullet,
Don Sirino Serna said to us, "Stand firm,
He left us a worthy example of civic valor."

Songs such as these give us the Tepoztecan definition of patriotism. The *patria* is the *patria chica*, the mountain-walled valleys of northern Morelos. In *Adelita* the soldier sings:

Soy soldado revolucionario
    Que defiendo el suelo en que nací
Porque no verlo en poder de otro extraño,
    Opresor que no sea del país.

I'm a soldier of the revolution
Who defends the soil where I was born,
So as not to see it in the power of some foreigner,
Some oppressor who is not of the country.

The appeal is always to the people of Morelos. "Morelenses! Hurrah for the plan of Ayala!" "Would they pass through thee, O State of Morelos?" And

the tendency in Morelos for this nationalistic consciousness to assume a racial aspect is indicated in

Que vivan los valientes defensores de la sierra,
Hurrah for the brave defenders of the sierra,

Que vivan nuestros jefes de la revolución,
Hurrah for our revolutionary leaders,

Que viva el Plan de Ayala, que vivan los aztecas,
Hurrah for the Plan of Ayala, hurrah for the Aztecs,

Muera Don Venustiano y su mal opinión.
Death to Don Venustiano and his bad cause.

This, then, is the real literature of Tepoztlán.[1] It
does not merely persist; it thrives and multiplies; it is
a true voice of the people. It is not Indian but Mexican. It is comparable with the ballads of fifteenth-
century England. In general it passes from the mouth
of the singer to the ear of the listener, who becomes
the next singer. But many *corridos* are written down.
It is easier to learn a song if you can borrow the text
and study it over. It is probable that one of the
earliest needs for writing felt by an illiterate *tonto* is
in connection with these songs. When such a one was
asked if he knew some songs, he replied regretfully,

[1] The classification of the local songs here used may be summarized:

    Traditional songs, ritualistic and anonymous
        Sacred songs of public ritual: *alabanzas*
        Secular songs of private ritual: *mañanitas*
    Ephemeral songs, social and aesthetic
        Conventional art forms
            Odes of love
            The singer sung
        More truly expressive songs, preserving group
            experience and defining group values
        Songs of war and heroism
            Soldier songs
            Political lampoons
            Narrative songs

"Oh, no, I have no copy-book." To know and to be able to sing the current songs is a common ambition of young boys. It is an advantage to be able to write. A girl of fourteen of the largely illiterate *barrio* of Los Reyes was the only one of her family to have a knowledge of writing. Although *corridos* are a part of a man's world, not a woman's, her elder brother was forced to ask her to help him in writing down a song he wanted to learn. Her prestige was correspondingly increased.

At the same time the supremacy of these local songs is not unchallenged. Songs of the city are occasionally heard in Tepoztlán. There are several phonographs, and these aid in making city songs popular. The songs of urban Mexico are much like our sentimental songs. As the urbanization of Tepoztlán slowly progresses, the city songs will become more usual; there will be a shift of emphasis from folk song to popular song.[1]

[1] One convention of city sentiment prevails in Tepoztlán. As elsewhere in Mexico, it is customary to give a person on his birthday colored postcards depicting white blonde women and men in European attire in attitudes of banal affection, amid turtledoves and flowers. These cards are as customary as the *mañanitas* on birthday mornings.

CHAPTER XI

THE *SANTO* AND THE *VETERANO*

It should appear from the foregoing chapter that the most important groups of songs, with the possible exception of the conventional love songs, are the *alabanzas* and the *corridos*.[1] The former are traditional, sacred, ritualistic; the latter are ephemeral, secular, and historical. But the *corridos* that recount the exploits of military heroes are like the *alabanzas* in this: they also are songs of celebration; they also extol personages that embody the admiration or adoration of the Tepoztecans. The one praises the *santo;* the other, the *veterano*. The *santo* and the *veterano* are both symbols of the ideals, the wishes, of the group. These symbols are local; in most instances the meaning that they have is for the locality only. The community is ideologically as well as economically self-sufficient.

The *santo* is a local patron. Each Indian village in pre-Columbian days had its patron deity, while in Mediterranean Europe protector gods of city or village were characteristic; it is impossible and unnecessary to say how much of each tradition enters into the attitudes of Tepoztlán. In rural Mexico every hamlet has its patron saint. In Tepoztlán, as has al-

[1] Using this word to mean the ballads describing current events or circumstances.

ready been stated,[1] each of the seven *barrios* has likewise its special protector. There are usually a number
of images in each church, but only one, usually en-
shrined in the principal altar, is the local guardian.
(In the chapels of the *barrios* there is often[2] only the
one image: that of the namesake and patron of the
barrio.) It is the particular effigy that is venerated;
reports[3] are plentiful of the refusal of the people to
accept a new effigy of the saint as at all the equivalent
of the old.

The people who live in the community presided over
by the *santo* have a particular and exclusive attitude
toward his protection. It is they primarily who make
offerings on his name day; and it is they who have the
task and the pleasure of maintaining his chapel, his
cornfield, and his vestments. And they are rewarded
with his special care. "San Sebastian," said a man of
that *barrio*, "is the most miraculous *santo* in Tepoztlán. Therefore we are the most fortunate *barrio*. He
appears to us in dreams and gives us advice."

Around these *santos* tend to cluster legends of their
miraculous power.

Our *santo* [of Santa Cruz] is very miraculous. Therefore we
venerate it. When the Carranzistas, during the revolution, tried
to break into the chapel, their bullets flattened on the door and
refused to enter. One man went in and started toward the altar.
He fell dead at the foot of the altar. It is a very miraculous

[1] Chap. iv.

[2] La Santa Cruz is one exception.

[3] Gamio, *La población del valle de Teotihuacan*, II, 215; Adan, art., "Las
danzas de Coatetelco."

image. It punishes too. If one does something evil, first one's children die, then oneself. But it does all we ask it in good faith. So we venerate it much.

Most of the *santos* receive veneration only in the locality. But when legends such as this cluster thickly, the image comes to be sought by people not of the region, and in this way develop the sacred shrines of Mexico, such as Guadalupe and Chalma. The Virgin of Guadalupe, with the universally known story of her miraculous apparition to an ordinary Indian, is the religious common denominator of Mexico. So at lesser shrines an individual may develop a special personal relation with a *santo* not his by inheritance. An Otomi Indian from north of Mexico City was in a village in the state of Puebla during the revolution. He attributed his escape from death in a serious engagement to the local *santo;* therefore he now makes occasional pilgrimages to her shrine. Such relationships are often entered into in times of crisis by a conditional vow which is essentially contractual.[1]

Neither the present materials nor those of Dr. Gamio indicate special personal relations between an individual and the *santo* on whose name day the individual is born, such as occur in Catholic Europe.

The word *santo* is special and exact; there is no substitute for it, and it is used in both Spanish and Nahuatl discourse. Generally it means any sacred effigy;

---

[1] Gamio (*op. cit.*, II, 217) prints the text of an actual written contract made by votaries intending to perform certain religious dances in exchange for the good will of the saint, the penalty for failure to perform the dances to be incarceration in the local jail.

specifically and commonly it refers to the images of Christian saints housed in temples. *Veterano*, on the other hand, is not a word with this precise conceptual connotation. It is an appellation applied to any distinguished military leader. People do not say *los veteranos* as they do say *los santos*. But the term always implies the heroic qualities which, tending to become mythical, make the *veterano* a symbol rather than an individual person; and, therefore, it is convenient to use it to denote this secular complement of the *santo*.

Every revolution produces its hundreds of *veteranos*. The memories of the lesser *veteranos* exert an influence as local as that of the lesser *santos*. The reputation of a few becomes as wide as Mexico. Probably the best known of these popular heroes is Pancho Villa,[1] and perhaps the one other who comes close to national fame is Emiliano Zapata. In spite of this wide notoriety, Zapata remains, however, a particular hero, and the greatest hero, of the Indians of Morelos. There live the memories of many other Zapatista generals— of Felipe Neri, Sirino Serna, Diego Ruiz, and Everardo González. There were at least five Zapatista generals from Tepoztlán.[2] There are stories about all of these, and *corridos* about many, but the heroic qualities of none of them can compare with the local conception of Emiliano Zapata, the principal leader of the southern revolutionary movement against Car-

[1] There are many *corridos* about Villa and several popular books describing his life and exploits.

[2] The three Sanchez brothers and the two Galvan brothers.

ranza. A Tepoztecan tells what he knows about Zapata in the following words:

Yes, I saw Zapata many times. He was a short, slender man with long black mustaches. I was sixteen years old during the revolution. It began this way. Zapata was a poor boy; they had nothing to eat in his house but *tortillas*. When he grew up he worked as a *peón*. After Díaz had to run away, Zapata began with no more than a dozen men who went with him to the hills. Then more joined him. But they had no money. The way he fed his soldiers was this: he would go to a *pueblo* and say, "We need so many *tortillas*, so much beans." The people were glad to bring them. Madero tried to betray Zapata, and on pretense of friendship was going to kill him. But Zapata would not be caught. When the people heard how Madero wanted to betray him, they rose in support of Zapata.

Once there was a battle in Tepoztlán between General Sanchez and the Carranzistas, and the Carranzistas were beaten. Sanchez was killed in an attack they made on a train at a station on the Balsas line they call La Cañada. That discouraged the Zapatistas. Everything grew calm again. But there was a time when Zapata held all the state, and for four months he was in Mexico City.

Zapata was killed by treason. General Guajardo, a Carranzista, sent word he would like to make an agreement with Zapata, by which he would go over to Zapata, and asked Zapata to meet him at the *hacienda* of Chinameca. Zapata accepted, and came with only twenty-five soldiers. Guajardo greeted him in a friendly way, and tried to get Zapata to drink with him. They had good beer brought all the way from Mexico, and of course *la mula*.[1] But Zapata would not drink. He went out with his men to make a circuit of the hills, to make sure there were no federal troops near. Guajardo kept reassuring him there was no danger; that his men were watching. When Zapata came back and entered the *portón*, Guajardo's men fired on him and he fell dead. But afterward Guajardo was killed by the Zapatistas.

[1] *Aguardiente.*

Zapata was a very great man. The only reason he lost was that he had no money. He fought for the poor people, but the millionaires were against him.

Zapata as a symbol embodies the group consciousness of the Indians of Morelos which developed during the revolution. His exploits are sung all over Mexico, but it is especially in Morelos that his memory is revered. *Corridos*[1] about him, written elsewhere in Mexico, describe his "base passions" and refer to him as "an Attila." But in the songs of the local collection he is "our defender," "a Napoleon," "our exalted savior," "the scourge of many a traitor," and "so wise and quick-thinking a *veterano*."

Les encargó a las fuerzas surianas	He charged the forces of the south
Que como jefe y sublime reden-	As chief and exalted savior;
tor;	
Su memoria conserven mañana	To preserve his memory tomorrow
Como prueba de su patrio amor.	As a proof of their love of country.

It is only in Morelos, in Tepoztlán and scores of Indian villages like it, that Zapata becomes truly legendary, and then even mythical. It is only in Morelos that he becomes a King Arthur, a Robin Hood. The stories and songs about Zapata may be dignified with the term "cycle." To the extent that these stories and songs merely keep alive a glorious memory they are legends—the folk counterpart of history. To the extent that the figure of Zapata defines the standards and justifies the conduct and ethical judgments of the people out of which he arose, they are myths.

[1] Obtained in printed form in Mexico City.

The substance of one local *corrido*, the "Bola de San Juan Chinameca," describing an exploit of Zapata, may be given to illustrate the memories that are relished in Tepoztlán and the idealization of the *veterano*. After a formal introduction the singer tells that on March 28 Zapata arrived at the *hacienda* of Chinameca,[1] of which the caretaker was a Spaniard, Carriles. Zapata, "always filled with passion," addresses Carriles.

Este fué impedido de unos tres mil pesos, Y en seguida les de.	Of him was demanded some three thousand *pesos*, And that he give it to them immediately.
"Luego en el momento," contestó Carriles, "Tres mil bolas les daré."	"Right away, right this moment," answered Carriles, "I'll give you three thousand bullets."

Zapata, having received this answer, arranges his forces and says, "Now, boys, lively when you hear the bugle." The *hacienda* is surrounded; the Spaniards are terrified.

Llegó el terrible Zapata Con justicia y razón; Habló con imperio, "Vengan con una hacha Y tiren este portón."	Arrived the terrible Zapata With justice and right; He spoke commandingly, "Come with an ax And batter down this door."

The door is opened; the Zapatistas enter.

Tembló la tierra ese día, Zapata entró	The earth trembled that day, Zapata entered. . . . .

[1] About twenty miles south of Cuauhtla in south-central Morelos.

Carriles is ferreted out "just as he was, in his stockings," and the story ends swiftly.

Les juntó toditos, y les dió las onze,[1]	He brought them all together, and gave them a drink,
Y hincados frente de una peña,	And kneeling in front of a rock,
"Besen esta cruz y toquen clarines de bronze,	"Kiss this cross and let bronze trumpets sound,
"Y griten, ¡Que muera España!"	"And cry, Die Spain!"
Viva el General Zapata,	Long live General Zapata,
Viva su fe, y su opinión,	Long live his faith, and his cause,
Porque se la propuesto morir por la patria,	Because he made up his mind to die for the country,
Como yo, por la nación.	As I, for the nation.

Zapata is already a legend, but he tends to become a myth. He is already a representative of the type of heroic figure, a King Arthur, a Jesse James. Around his memory clings an aura of the miraculous. There are as yet no stories of his magical birth or parentage; perhaps they will come in time. He had, however, an inexplicable faculty of escaping his enemies, and he was equipped with a horse with powers that were supernatural.

Zapata was miraculously clever at escaping. He was many times surrounded but he always got away. One day he was penned into a house by the federals. The only entrance was by the *zaguán*, where there were federal troops. The wall at the back of the house was as high as that shelf [about seven feet]. Zapata had a wonderful horse. It was called Relámpago ["Lightning"]. When the federal troops were about to close in on him, he drove his spurs into Relámpago and leaped the wall—he was gone, none knew where.

When he came into a *pueblo* with his forces they always tried

[1] "It struck eleven for them"—a localism.

to find a house, oh, very clean [*muy limpiacita*], for him to sleep in. When he was sleeping no one might enter except his orderly. But many times Zapata would get up in the middle of the night and go and sleep under some rock in some secret place. None knew how he got there. Thus, though many times the federals surrounded the house where he slept, he always got away.

At the time of these investigations the "mythification" of Zapata had reached the point where the rumor was current that Zapata had escaped death at Chinameca and was still alive. *Corridos* of the reportorial type, written outside of Morelos shortly after the event and still current, describe the actual facts. The trap was set and sprung at Chinameca and Zapata was shot down by the soldiers of Jesús Guajardo on April 9, 1919. His body was exhibited in Cuauhtla to thousands; his tomb there is still a place of pilgrimage. Nevertheless the story current in Morelos among the Zapatistas is that it was another man who was killed. In the summer of 1926 a singer of that region put the story into a *corrido*, which begins:

Han publicado, los cantadores,	They have spread, those singers,
Una mentira fenomenal,	An extraordinary lie,
Y todos dicen que ya Zapata	And everybody says that now Zapata
Descansa en paz en la eternidad.	Rests in eternal peace.
Pero si Ustedes me dan permiso	But if you will give me permission
Y depositan confianza en mi,	And rest your trust in me,
Voy a cantarles lo mas preciso,	I am going to tell you the exact truth,
Para informarles tal como ví.	So as to let you know just how I saw it.

The ballad goes on to tell how Pablo Gonzáles, a Carranzista general, when he learned that Zapata had gone to San Juan Chinameca, summoned Jesús Guajardo and with him developed the plan to send Guajardo to Zapata with the proposal that Guajardo turn Zapatista and deliver his forces and funds to the southern leader. Zapata then professed interest, and responded to Guajardo with an invitation to meet him at dinner. But Zapata knew that a trap was laid for him.

Como Zapata es tan veterano,	As Zapata is such a veteran,
Sagaz y listo para pensar,	Wise and quick witted,
Ya había pensado de ante mano	He had already thought beforehand
Mandar otro hombre en su lugar.	To send another man in his place.

So to one Jesús Delgado are given the coat, breeches, and leggings of Zapata, and he rides forth to die for Zapata.

Estado arriba, le dijo a su compadre,	Arrived at the top, he said to his companion,
"Hoy si estamos en la perdición,	"Now indeed we are lost,
¡Adiós, México, mi patria libre,	Farewell, Mexico, my free country,
¡Adiós, adiós, mi fiel nación!	Farewell, farewell, my true country!"
Le salió el tiro por la culata,	The shot came out through the back,[1]
Es positivo y no hay que dudar,	It is certain and cannot be doubted,
Pues se engañaron porque a Zapata,	But they were deceived about Zapata,
Ni una razón le han de poder dar.	They cannot put Zapata down.

[1] "They were fooled."

At about the same time as first appeared this *corrido* a soldier of Zapata in Tepoztlán gave his version of the matter in the following words:

It is not known whether Zapata still lives or whether he really was killed as reported. Some say he is in Arabia, and will return when he is needed. For myself, I think he still lives. I know he had a scar on his cheek, and the corpse that was brought back from Chinameca had no scar. I saw it myself. It is said Zapata knew the danger he was in, and had another put on his clothes and go out to die for him. He himself is in hiding, and still lives. He will come back when he is needed.

In this version the wish of the Zapatistas has found expression in the added element that looks to the future—the idea that some day the hero will return. Thus are justified the group consciousness and latent political ambitions of the Zapatistas. The story is now more than a memory, more than a legend; it is a myth.

CHAPTER XII
THE FOLK IN A CITY WORLD

In Mexico, as in European countries with more or less illiterate peasant populations, the sharpest cultural differences are not between one region and another but between the city people and the country people. This difference is, of course, even greater in those Latin-American countries where the city people derive their traditions from, and continue to communicate with, the European world, while the country people are largely Indian in tradition and do not easily communicate with the city. It is a circumstance of importance that the same classes, based upon the degree of familiarity with city ways, exist, on a much smaller scale, in Tepoztlán. They have already been several times referred to in these pages as *los correctos* and *los tontos*. The periodic revolutions afford, it would seem, a mechanism whereby this difference between the classes is from time to time re-emphasized and the tendency for them to merge is checked.

It is probable that these classes have existed for centuries in Tepoztlán. Tradition says that Martin Cortés, son of the conqueror, lived for a time in Tepoztlán and used the chapel of La Santísima as his private oratory. Certain heavy stone walls and ruined arches across the street from this chapel are pointed out as the vestiges of his residence. When he and his

dependents came there, they must at once have con-
stituted an aristocracy of Spanish culture. This must
have been but one of a series of periods of development and partial sophistication that were successively
interrupted by periods of disorder. There are other
fragments of heavy wall at the north side of the town;
all memories of their meaning have apparently disappeared. The latest of these eras of order and urbanization was coincident with the Díaz régime. In
the middle of the nineteenth century a family of educated people moved to Tepoztlán from another state.
This family contributed the priest, a teacher, and
several other members of the Tepoztecan intelligentsia. During this period the first secular school was
opened. Several attempts were made to publish local
newspapers.[1] In 1895 Francisco Rodriguez, a Tepoztecan who was educated as an engineer, called the attention of the scientific world to the large pre-Columbian temple situated above the town, and reported
upon it to the International Congress of Americanists.[2] The work of excavation was done largely by
Tepoztecan volunteers. A museum was established in

[1] "More than a half a century ago, nevertheless, literary productions were
published in Tepoztlán; nevertheless, the press has hardly been introduced to the
population. We remember, for example, 'El Xocoyotzin' of Don José Guadalupe
Rojas,—a man never well understood,—a small periodical which was devoted to
adult and infant education. A little later, with the introduction of a press in
1882, appeared in the public light 'El Liliputiense,' 'El Mosquito,' 'El Grano de
Arena' and still others which were devoted to the development of culture and the
illumination of the people" (*El Tepozteco*, a newspaper published by Tepoztecos
in Mexico City in 1921, issue of October 1).

[2] F. Rodriguez, art., ":Descripción de la pyramide llamada Casa del Tepozteco. . . . ."

one of the public buildings. German and North American scientists visited the archaeological ruins and incidentally the town; indeed, the railroad ran special excursion trains to El Parque.

This period of brilliance, like, no doubt, other earlier periods of the sort, was terminated by revolution—that of 1910. Perhaps no other part of Mexico was so swept by the fury of war as was Morelos. For years this state was the scene of sanguinary encounters between Zapatistas and Carranzistas. The railroads were torn up, the sugar mills destroyed, and most of the cattle exterminated. During almost two years Tepoztlán was entirely depopulated except when federal or Zapatista troops occupied the town. Almost all the more substantial houses were partly or entirely destroyed. The little museum was wrecked and its contents scattered. After people began to return, there was a long period of suffering from famine and sickness.[1]

[1] A Zapatista soldier who spent eight years in the campaign, part of this time in the neighborhood of Tepoztlán, his home, described the period thus: "In the time of the revolution, for a long period, Tepoztlán was entirely depopulated. The people went to Mexico, or to the hills. The hills north of the town are full of caves where people lived. Some built lean-tos of cornstalks under big trees. For a time there was enough food. We used to come down from the hills at night to get corn. If there was anybody in the town, it would be Federal troops. We would go very quietly, listening. If we heard nothing, we entered and took the corn. The people who owned fruit trees would come down from the hills by night to rob their own trees.

"The hills were the populated places, the towns the wild places. So we went into the towns to hunt. One day we were out of food. My colonel asked me and some others to get a deer. But I said, 'There are no more deer in the hills. We must go to the towns for a deer.' So we went down into Santiago and there, among the banana trees, we found and killed a deer.

"Later on the food gave out. The cows and bulls had been hunted down and

During this period there were no civilians in Tepoztlán. Many of the men joined the forces of Zapata.
To those who did not was presented the choice of flee-
ing to the hills or of going to one of the cities, usually
Mexico City, where security was greater. The people
who were already used to the city and who were more
likely to have friends there and to have the money
necessary to become established there, went to the city.
The poorer people, who were also those least used to
city ways, were the ones who went to the hills. Hill
exile was a life of isolation, a life of rumor, of reliance
upon the most primitive techniques of maintenance.[1]

---

killed; the corn was eaten up. If an orange was found it was taken quickly and
eaten green. Many, many died of hunger, both soldiers and non-combatants.
When, after this time, food was obtained again, some died because they ate too
much. We began with a half a *tortilla* at a time, and so escaped death from gorg-
ing."

[1] A *tonto* of the *barrio* of San Sebastian tells of his experiences: "Times were
very horrible during the revolution. At first people stayed in Tepoztlán. J. C.
[a *correcto*] was not there, but his father stayed at first, until it grew too bad; and
then he too went to Mexico City. Tepoztlán was deserted for two years. The
soldiers came and ate the corn, and killed all the animals. The Carranzistas killed
what they didn't want to eat; not an animal was left. The troops came at last to
eat dogs and cats, there was so little food. No one was safe. Many were killed,
and not even buried. If the Carranzistas saw anyone, they shot him without any
question.

"Many went to the cities, some to the hills. I went to the hills with my family. There were my father, my mother, and seven brothers. I was sixteen. We
lived in a cave in the heights, in that direction [toward Yautepec]. We took the
metates along. But we had no animals; we carried everything ourselves. We
lived by what food we could find in the hills or in the towns, and by what we
could sell in Mexico City. We used to carry fruit to Mexico to sell. Fruit was
very expensive there. We sold limes at ten *pesos* a hundred. If you could just
get a hold of a thousand limes and bring them to Mexico City, you had a hundred
pesos. We took avocados too. We traveled only at night. It took two nights.
When dawn came we camped somewhere in the hills beyond Tres Marías.
Xochimilco was the bad place to go through; the Carranzistas waited there and
killed many. We brought back soap and salt.

"Then the fever came. Three of my brothers died. Bury them there? No, we

City exile brought the *émigrés* into competition with the people of the city, and so further sophisticated them. So it was that when after a period of years the inhabitants returned to rebuild their homes the difference between *tontos* and *correctos* had in the meantime been made more distinct.

These periods of exodus to the city render acute the growing self-consciousness of *los correctos*. *Los tontos* live, in spite of revolutions, in the same single mental world of the folk culture. *Los correctos*, on the other hand, develop an intelligentsia who live in two worlds, in two cultures, the city and the folk, and are correspondingly restless and often unhappy. The periods of revolution[1] sharpen the self-consciousness of this intelligentsia; drawn together as temporary expatriates, they idealize their home community and at the same time deprecate its shortcomings. This dissatisfaction and unrest finds an expression in programs of reform.

In April, 1920, the expatriated Tepoztecos in Mex-

---

brought them to the cemetery at Tepoztlán. We came down by night. It took about four hours. We took turns carrying the body. We had to bury without coffins, just *petates*. We made three such trips, each time getting back to the hills before dawn.

"Afterward, when people came back to Tepoztlán, all the animals had been killed and there was no corn left. Many died of hunger and the sickness came. Eight or nine died each day. P. R. lived in the house just across from us in San Sebastian. He was killed in the revolution. He left his wife and seven little children. They all died one after another. They wanted just a *tortilla*, but there wasn't enough.

[1] A minor period of decline occurred in 1928. Residents of Tepoztlán who belonged to the radical agrarian party started a local rebellion in which Tepoztecans were killed. Rebel activity was general in Morelos, and some Tepoztecan *correctos* went to the city.

ico City formally organized themselves into a "Colonia Tepozteco." The prospectus of this organization announced the chief program of the group: to supplant the then-existing military government of Tepoztlán with one elected by the people. The aims of the society were further specified as follows:

I. To establish among the Tepoztecos a center of intercourse which may contribute to the moral progress of its members.

II. To work for the reconstruction and the improvement, moral and material, of the *Municipalidad* of Tepoztlán.

III. To devote special attention to the spread of public education to the end that illiteracy no longer exists in Tepoztlán, employing for this result, without prejudice to the perfection of the Castilian language, the Nahuatl or Mexican idiom, an efficacious means of bringing the masses of the people to understand the transcendence of civilization, and, furthermore, to bring it about that our native tongue be preserved for transmission to the future generations.

IV. To develop a broad civic propaganda so that all Tepoztecan citizens recognize their rights and duties; and

V. To take a direct interest, moral and practical, in the designation of the local authorities of the *pueblo*, so as to realize the aspirations of the Colony.

In September of the same year a *fiesta* was celebrated in a hired hall in Mexico. A daughter of a leading *correcto*, expatriate in the capital, recited a poem about Tepoztlán written by her father. In this the beauties of the valley are hymned, the tragedy of ruin described, and the hopes of the future announced.

Mas tengo fe: las ruinas	Yet I have faith: the ruins
Subirán a los espacios,	Will rise to the empyrean,
Sus bases serán topacios,	Their foundations will be topazes,
Sus murallas diamantinas.	Their walls diamonds.

Con fuerzas casi divinas,	With strength almost divine,
Tepoztlán en su ardimiento,	Tepoztlán, courageous,
Sus ideales, su aliento	Its ideals, its vigor,
Desplegará con nobleza;	Will unfold nobly;
Si es titánica la empresa,	If the enterprise is titanic,
Es titan su pensamiento.	The thought is a Titan.

In October, 1921, this same group of intellectuals issued a tiny newspaper, *El Tepozteco*, with the motto: *"Nochi ipampa totlacatiliztlal"* ("All for our native land"). This short-lived periodical[1] contained no news, but only editorial sermons on sobriety, patriotism, and especially on reform in Tepoztlán. The editor addressed his compatriots under the *nom de plume* Cihtli-Tepoztecatl ("Paternal Ancestor the Tepoztecan"), writing in the rôle of the eponymous legendary chief returned to advise his people:

> I come to be with you, to arouse you to the titanic emprise of the reconstruction of our *pueblo;* I come to applaud the strength you may exert so that my Tepoztlán may once again be what it was in the decade past; I come to anathematize those evil compatriots of mine, who, with their apathy or selfish ideas of conflict, obstruct the labor of the good citizens; and I come, finally, to be as I have always been, the mythological personage of our history and of our race .... [*El Tepozteco*].

This developing group consciousness is a product of conflict; it is apparently most acute in those individuals who, coming to live in the world of the city, look back upon the world of the folk. The impulse for reform, just described, has much in common with the nationalistic movements of folk minorities of Europe. The phenomenon in Tepoztlán, in the development of

[1] The writer does not know that more than the one issue appeared.

a native intelligentsia, in the local press, in political ambition, and especially in the linguistic revival, repeats a process that has occurred in many another place where the folk have felt the impact of the city. The pride in the native tongue to a certain extent is shared even by the *tontos*. Among the *correctos* it is more definitely expressed in attempts to keep alive and indeed to "purify" (i.e., to eliminate Spanish loanwords and forms) the beloved tongue. Several attempts have been made in Tepoztlán to organize schools, or discussion groups, for the study and development of Nahuatl. An early leader in this movement is Mariano J. Rojas, native Tepoztecan, now professor of Nahuatl in Mexico City.[1] But several other *correctos* who remain in Tepoztlán assiduously cultivate the language and have attempted to maintain a sort of academy of native speech. The romantic idealization of the language and how it symbolizes local patriotism appear from the following paragraph, published in *El Tepozteco:*

The sweet and sonorous idiom of our aborigines, of Nezahual-coyotl and Ixtlilxochitl, the idiom of our fathers, which was left us as a sacred heritage, shall not die in spite of those who, although physically they reveal an origin entirely Indian, are ashamed of their race; our language shall live, because there are great and patriotic citizens who do not look down upon their race, who glory in being Indian, who love the members of their race, who greatly esteem their native tongue, and who work, toil and exert themselves for its reconstruction and perfection so that it shall never die.

[1] Author of *Manual de la lengua Nahuatl.*

This use of the language as a symbol of the Indian heritage has helped to give the movement a racial rather than a nationalistic character.

After the revolution of 1910–23 few of *los correctos* returned to Tepoztlán. Most of those who did go back went back to employ the practical and commercial experience they had acquired in the city in order to earn a living in Tepoztlán. They are the artisans and merchants there today. Of the six men who were most instrumental in organizing the colony of Tepoztecan *émigrés*—the group of intelligentsia—only one returned. Except two teachers, he was the only real intellectual living in Tepoztlán at the time of these observations. The substance of his life-history gives in a specific case the experience passed through by that type of individual who springs from the folk, is no longer entirely at home in it and yet can never quite leave it, and who suffers the conflict and disorganization of his position, with one foot in one world and the other foot in another.[1]

R. G. was born in Tepoztlán about forty-six years ago. He is apparently a pure-blooded Indian. His father was poor, but, like the other Tepoztecans, had his *milpa*. He was a man of some education, and, after the federal government had taken charge of the pre-Columbian ruins above the town, he was made "keeper of the monuments" at three *pesos* a day. The son, R., lived in Tepoztlán until he was nineteen years old. Up to that time his only schooling was that of the little local public school. In his own words, he "lived like an animal," running about and having a good time with the other boys but with no ideas or aims direct-

[1] Dr. Robert E. Park has called this type the "marginal man" (art., "Migration and the Marginal Man").

ed toward any other interests than those offered by the ordinary life of the town. At the age of nineteen he was sent by his father to school in Cuernavaca. A great many of *los correctos* have studied in Cuernavaca. Because of the tourists and its position on the railroad and the fact that it is the seat of the state government, Cuernavaca is far more sophisticated than Tepoztlán. R. G. studied in the secondary school there. Evidently his interest in study was aroused, for he then went on to a normal school in Mexico City.

In Mexico City one of the ruling passions of his life—his interest in the Nahuatl language—had its origin through a friendship he picked up with a North American priest and amateur archaeologist. To R. G., Nahuatl had been with Spanish equally the language of intimate home life. But through the archaeologist he received a Nahuatl grammar and from him he first made acquaintance with the literature describing the past glories of his Aztec forbears. The Nahuatl language became for him a symbol of gradually developing race consciousness. He entered into discussions with the archaeologist on the ancient forms of the language and studied it with the idea of bringing back to use the sacred pure original forms.

He had made only brief stays in Tepoztlán when the revolution broke out, and was of course in Mexico City all during that period. He took an active share in organizing the "Colonia Tepozteco," and entered enthusiastically into the plans for the restoration and reform of Tepoztlán. All during this time he was employed at various clerical occupations. During the early years of the revolution he met and married a *mestiza* woman, part Tarascan Indian, part Spanish. Although he is apparently proud of his pure Indian blood, he married a woman lighter skinned and closer to the Spanish tradition than himself. At about the same time he became acquainted with the authorities in charge of anthropological work for the government, and was employed in a minor capacity in connection with the work of that department. When he was asked to take part in an ancient Aztec pageant which the department had arranged as a part of the deliberate revival of the ancient cultural traditions of the folk, R. G. refused indignantly to make himself ridiculous by dressing up in feathers. He offered instead to write and deliver an oration in Nahuatl pointing out the beauties of the Nahuatl language.

By the time the revolution was over R. G. had four children. Their situation in Mexico City was fairly comfortable. But he was only one of a mass of low-paid white-collar employees with little opportunity to gain recognition now that the Tepoztecan colony was broken up, and he had felt more intensely than most the desires to, as he put it, "lift up my homeland out of the sink into which it has fallen." Just then his father, who was living in Tepoztlán as "keeper of the monuments," died, and R. G. asked for and secured the post for himself. He returned to Tepoztlán, to the job, the house, and the *milpa* of his father. In spite of the misgivings of his wife, who is a city person and had moreover her own family in Mexico City, he transported himself and family, a few pieces of furniture, and the Nahuatl grammar to the mud-floored, windowless *adobe* house that had been his birthplace. He launched at once into his efforts at civic reform, promoting new roads, new street lights, and a school for the instruction of Nahuatl. He met with the apathy and often open amusement of his townspeople. The practical reforms ended with the installation of a few gasoline lamps. The school failed because, he says, "it was opposed by the priest." In Mexico City R. G. had become an atheist and anticlerical. He was equally out of sympathy with the small radical political group, who are *tontos*.

By the end of his fifth year in Tepoztlán he was thoroughly uncomfortable in both body and soul. His wife, suffering from the hardships of the primitive mode of life, was an invalid, dragging herself out of bed in order to do the necessary work about the house. She was extremely isolated, for she had not been able to adjust or interest herself in the life of the town. Her only desire was to get back to Mexico City. Her husband, a more sanguine person, was at times hopeful and passionately enthusiastic, at times profoundly disillusioned. To himself he is a figure in Tepoztlán, but one who goes unrecognized; and toward *los tontos* he maintains an attitude which some of them feel to be patronizing and critical, while he moves among them making elaborate jokes in Nahuatl. He is a lively, agreeable person but sensitive and proud. He is disillusioned, yet he continues to hope for the

Tepoztecan millennium. At bottom his attitudes are those of other Tepoztecans, but all is overlaid and colored by self-consciousness, and by a consciousness of the world outside not shared by his neighbors. During the sickness of one of his children he put equal weight on folk and city medicine. He laughs at *los aires*, but like his neighbors he thinks it unsafe to sleep out of doors; for him, however, it is because "germs drop from trees."

In 1926 the death of two of his children and a minor revolutionary disturbance in Morelos provided the occasion for his departure for Mexico City. In so doing he abandoned his dreams and forsook his status. But a partial transfer of desires has taken place; he talks now of learning English and coming to the United States. There one can make money, and there scientists are interested in his language.

R. G. can be understood partly in terms of his particular temperament, but partly in the light of that development of racial and national consciousness that has so marked the last two decades in Mexico. As he sees Tepoztlán partly through the eyes of a man of the wider city-world, so are the folk of Mexico coming to see themselves. His dreams and despairs, his crudities and his sensitiveness, are those of his country.

CHAPTER XIII

THE INTERMEDIATE COMMUNITY

The culture of Tepoztlán appears to represent a type intermediate between the primitive tribe and the modern city. It has, one would venture, its nearest analogues in the peasant communities of the more backward parts of Europe, of the Near East, and of the Orient. To the extent that Tepoztlán is economically and mentally self-sufficient, to the extent that its social heritage is local and is transmitted without the use of writing, to the extent that all knowledge is intimate and personal and is closely associated with the ancient habitat of the people, the community resembles a primitive tribe. But just to the degree that Tepoztlán conceives itself as a part of the outside world, and that the Tepoztecans define their personal problems in terms of modern city civilization, it is unlike a tribal society. The Tepoztecans are primarily Tepoztecans, but they are also, if somewhat more remotely, Mexicans. Their society might be called a "folk" community, in a more special sense than that in which the term is often used.

So little, outside of the material culture, are elements of pre-Columbian custom preserved that it presents small opportunity to a culture historian interested in the character of the aboriginal society.

Only from the point of view of history or of romantic appreciation is Tepoztlán an "Aztec *pueblo*." The elaborate ritual and philosophic scheme which distinguished the pre-Columbian culture was carried by the priestly class; and these meanings were practically extirpated by the conquerors. The society was, one might say, decapitated. The ancient household techniques remain, but the ancient values are gone.

But if the interest is not in depiction, but in studying social change as it takes place—in social anthropology as contrasted with ethnology, in the terminology of Radcliffe-Brown[1]—then Tepoztlán presents an excellent opportunity. This opportunity is for the study of the change whereby a folk community is slowly becoming more like the city. This change is a case of diffusion, occurring in an easily observed situation, so slowly as not to accomplish the disorganization of the community, and under practical circumstances which liberate the student from responsibility to record the fragmentary vestiges of a disappearing culture.

The frontier of this change is between *los correctos* and *los tontos*. This frontier is a geographical, not merely a figurative, frontier. The diffusion of city traits can be observed and expressed in spatial terms. The point from which changes originate is the central *plaza*. This is at first confusing to one accustomed to examples of the diffusion process taken from tribal

[1] A. R. Radcliffe-Brown, art., "The Methods of Ethnology and Social Anthropology."

societies. There the changes that originate in the center of an area are those modifications locally developed in accordance with the characteristic type of the area, while the changes that take place because of contact with another culture take place on the periphery. But here, with a paradox that is only apparent, the periphery of change is at the center. This is because the contact with the city takes place here. Here visitors come. Here are trade, machinery, and print, so far as these come at all to Tepoztlán. And here, by a sort of selection, are drawn the tradespeople whose rôles have been determined by urban competition and who are familiar with city ways. These people—the tradespeople and other *correctos*—on the one hand, communicate by direct face-to-face relations with *los tontos* on the periphery, and, on the other hand, through their memories of the city, and by means of letters, newspapers, and visits to the capital, communicate with the city. It is as though there were, in this central zone where live *los correctos*,[1] two overlapping culture "areas": a culture of the folk, with communication by direct contact, and a culture of the city, which impinges on the other culture in another dimension, by means of communication which transcends space.

The ways of the city diffuse outward from the central *plaza*. They are not carried outward by migration, because the interests and activities of *los correc-*

[1] Of course there is no definite zone, but merely a tendency for *los correctos* to dwell, and for city traits to occur, near the *plaza* rather than near the outskirts.

tos cause them to live near the *plaza* and so keep out *los tontos*, and also because people continue to occupy the house sites of their ancestors. By spotting the traits on a map of the community the distribution of city traits as compared with folk traits could be indicated. An example of such a distribution is given on the accompanying map. Here are contrasted the distributions of two sorts of professionals. Each letter indicates the home (except in a few cases this is also the place of business) of an individual with a recognized specialty. On the one hand are those specialists —tradespeople and artisans—who practice European techniques and who mostly acquired their specialties through economic competition. These are in general found near the *plaza*. On the other hand are the midwives, herb doctors, and fireworks-makers, who practice more ancient, traditional techniques and who in more cases came into their rôles by birth. These tend to be found toward the periphery.

The upper three *barrios*, San Pedro, Los Reyes, and San Sebastian (and, to a somewhat less extent, Santa Cruz), are the most remote from the *plaza* and are *barrios* of *tontos*. These three contain the greatest proportionate number of magical specialists and not a single rational specialist of the sorts listed. The people in these *barrios* have a different "mentality" from those that dwell around the *plaza*. Racially they are no different, but the experiences they undergo are different. They are "timeless" for one thing; few up there have watches, and they are too far away to hear the clock on the *plaza*. Illiteracy is greater up there. The mailcarrier in the months of these observations never delivered a letter to one of these three *barrios*.

These statements, and those that follow, need of course the support of a more substantial body of materials and more careful exploration into the facts. They are made merely to define a problem for further work. In this sense it may be stated that the distributions of various aspects of city ways rather strikingly coincide. Those elements of material culture which were more recently taken over from the city and are still exterior to the Spanish-Indian folk culture, such as forks, felt hats, and metal beds, are to be found in the inner zone of *los correctos*. Here also is most marked the tendency toward secularization of holiday celebration. It is *los correctos* who promote the carnival, with its strongly secularized, commercialized aspect; while it is *los tontos* who control the religious *fiestas*, with their greater detail of ritual and remoteness from commercial activity. The three most important *fiestas* commemorating *santos* occur respectively in San Pedro, San Sebastian, and Ixcatepec, on the peripheries of the community. It is *los tontos* who preserve the most traditional ritual on practical occasions of crisis, such as birth or death. One might venture to guess that the nearer a birth occurs to the central *plaza* the less the proportion of merely ritualistic, expressive behavior and the greater the proportion of purely practical behavior which attends the occasion.

If the difference between *los correctos* and *los tontos* increases during periods of disorder, it decreases during periods of peace. And during these latter times the progressive advance of city ways, the influence of *los correctos* over *los tontos*, can be observed. This process, it has already been sufficiently suggested, is a process of diffusion. It remains only to point out that this diffusion process may be thought of somewhat more broadly than is usually possible in the instances of diffusion ordinarily considered by ethnologists, where the bare facts have to be reconstructed or learned at second hand.

In the first place, it may be supposed that the diffusion is not merely the communication, between contemporary groups, of the traits usually listed, of technique and ritual. There pass also what can rather awkwardly be called "subjective" traits: mental form as well as mental content. It is not merely that the group comes to employ a new artifact or to adopt a new attitude toward marriage or toward a religious practice. It may be said that the whole mentality correspondingly changes, if by "mentality" is understood a complex of habits employed in meeting unfamiliar problems. Mentality in this sense too is an aspect of culture. If the individual undergoes experiences of a very different sort from those undergone before, he develops a correspondingly new organ, a new mind. The patterns of thinking of a city man, where a multitude of unfamiliar experiences are dealt with by relegating them to convenient classes, are different from those of a remote rural dweller whose social objects are all unique and known by their individual characters. So, if it can be shown that *los correctos* tend to reject traditional magical ways of curing disease, for instance, and accept instead the ways of modern life, it might be that such a change be not entirely due to the prestige of city cures but due also to a general tendency to solve problems by means wherein the mechanisms involved are understood.

In the second place, the diffusion is not merely the borrowing of ethnological traits, because the diffusion is accompanied by a change in the attitude which the people have toward themselves. The just-preceding chapter suggests that a study of diffusion here is not merely enumerating elements of culture which the group has or has not, but also involves a consideration of striking changes in the type of personality to be expected in the group. The sensitiveness, pride, and zeal for reform which characterize the individual described in that chapter are perhaps traits that typify the culture of his group (*los correctos*), but they were not borrowed from the city. They are changes which have resulted in him out of the conflict between the two cultures in which, mentally, he is living at the same time. The way a people feel about themselves and about other people is a datum which may be included in a direct study, such as this might be, of the culture process.

APPENDIX A
RELATIONSHIP TERMS

The terms in use in Tepoztlán, when Nahuatl is spoken, are the same (with occasional minor variations) as they were in ancient Nahuatl, according to the list extracted from Molina (*Vocabulario de la lengua mexicana*, 1571) by Paul Radin,[1] in the following instances: "son," "father," "mother," "grandfather," "grandson" ("granddaughter"?), "son-in-law," and "daughter-in-law." These ancient terms had the same specific connotation in old Nahuatl. But where the old language made age or other distinctions not recognized by European kinship terminology, such terms disappeared and were replaced by Spanish terms in modern Tepoztecan Nahuatl vocabulary, or else were extended to cover the class represented by the nearest Spanish term. The former change is illustrated by the use of Spanish terms for "nephew," "niece," "brother-in-law," "sister-in-law," and "cousin" (general classifications which the old Nahuatl did not make) and by the new (?) general Nahuatl word for "brother" or "sister" (*icnihtli*). The latter change is represented by the extension of *nonnantli* to mean the husband's mother as well as the wife's mother, and the corresponding extension of the word for "wife's father." It is not clear why the Spanish words for "uncle" and "aunt" appear to have superseded, in Tepoztlán, the old Nahuatl terms. Perhaps these were individualizing rather than classificatory. The modern words for "husband" and "wife" are likewise different, but probably are also old terms (*nozoa* means simply "my woman").

The terms in the following table are given as they appear when standing alone. Actually they are usually heard with the pronominal particle and hence without the suffix; but often with the honorific suffix. Thus *pilli* is almost never heard, but *nopiltzin* ("my child"), etc.; so *nocihtzin*, not *cihtli*, etc. So it is also with Spanish terms used in Nahuatl discourse (but the honorific is not added): *nosuegra* ("my mother-in-law").

[1] "Maya, Nahuatl and Tarascan Kinship Terms."

English	Tepoztecan Nahuatl	Ancient Aztec Nahuatl
Father..............	*Tata, tatzin*	Same
Mother..............	*Nana, nantzin*	Same
Son or daughter......	*Pilli, conetl*	Same [Radin gives *tepiltzin* or *noconeuh,* "son"; *yacapantli* or *teconeuh,* "daughter"]
Brother or sister......	*Icnihtli*	[No word for "brother" or "sister," but words for "older brother," "younger brother," "older sister," "younger sister"]
Grandfather..........	*Colli*	Same
Grandmother.........	*Cihtli*	Same
Grandson............	*Ixhuitli*	Same [also meant "father's brother's son"]
Granddaughter.......	?	*Texiuh*
Uncle...............	"*Tio*"	*Tlahtli*
Aunt................	"*Tia*"	*Auitl*
Nephew.............	"*Sobrino*"	[No general word for "nephew"; *ixhuitl* designated "father's brother's son"]
Niece...............	"*Sobrina*"	[No general word for "niece"; *teixiuh* designated "father's brother's daughter"]
Cousin..............	"*Primo*"	[No general word for "cousin"; children of father's brother designated by special terms; other cousins distinguished according to whether older or younger than the speaker]
Mother-in-law........	*Nonnantli* or "*Suegra*"	*Nonnantli* designated "wife's mother" only
Father-in-law........	*Montahtli* or "*Suegro*"	*Montahtli* designated "wife's father" only
Brother-in-law........	"*Cuñado*"	*Textli* [*tehuextli?*] designated the wife's brother [or wife's sister]
Sister-in-law.........	"*Cuñada*"	*Uezatli* designated only the "husband's sister"
Son-in-law...........	*Montli*	Same
Daughter-in-law......	*Zoamontli*	Same (variant form, *cihuamontli*)
Husband.............	*Namictli*	*Teoquichui*
Wife................	*Zoatli*	*Teciuauh*

English	Tepoztecan Nahuatl	Ancient Aztec Nahuatl
Stepfather............	*Tlacpatahtli*	?
Stepmother..........	*Chahuanantli*	?
Godfather............	"*Padrino*," less commonly, *toyotahtli*	....
Godmother..........	"*Madrina*," less commonly, *toyonantli*	....
Reciprocal term used between parents and godparents, between two godparents of the same child, or, by extension, to any intimate friend........	"*Compadre*" (used in both Spanish and Nahuatl discourse)	....
Reciprocal term used between the two pairs of parents-in-law [Sp. *consuegros*].........	*Huexihtli*	?
Reciprocal term used between individuals who bear the same baptismal name [Sp. *hermanos de nombre*].	*tocaihnihtli*	?

APPENDIX B
TEXT OF *RELACION*

[The following is a part of the Nahuatl text of the *relación*, used at the *fiesta* Altepe-ilhuitl in September, which is spoken by the actor representing "El Tepozteco." A somewhat different version, including a short reply made in turn by each of the attacking *pueblos*, has been collected and published by Robelo.[1] The first line of the following extract is the text as I collected it, suffering from the degeneration of long traditional use and the errors of the collector. The second line is the text as "restored" by Mr. John H. Cornyn, and the third line is Mr. Cornyn's translation. Mr. Cornyn says that the text was composed in the sixteenth century "on the model of the pre-Conquest Aztec metrical poetry (and) is written in the trochaic meter." He says also that "the Tepozteco or Lord of Tepoztlán accompanied the wizards and wonderworkers of Cuernavaca summoned to Mexico City by Moctezuma II, in the hope that they might prevent the arrival of the Spanish invaders to Tenochtitlan. He was one of the first converts to Christianity. For this reason the four cities mentioned in the text, so tradition says, rose against him; but, with the help of the Virgin, he defeated them and brought their lords and nobles into the Catholic fold. This incident was taken advantage of by Fr. Domingo de la Asunción, first missionary to Tepoztlán, to convert the heathen autumn festival into a Christian feast with its accompanying miracle play to replace the old ritual." The notes which follow the text were also kindly furnished by Mr. Cornyn.—R. R.]

Aquin anmehuatin nican anhuallahque ahueli
Aquin amehuantin nican anhuallaque[2] [o-huallaque]? Ahuel'[3] [ca amo]

                Not even

Who [are] you [who] have come here?

 [1] Art., "Diccionario de mitología Nahoa," pp. 228–34.

 [2] *An-huallaque* for *o-huallaque*. The poets frequently left out the sign of the preterite.

 [3] *Ahueli* is dialectic for *ca amo*, "not even."

227

antetlahpalchque; zan anhual cahcalactahque que anitzquintototin
antetlahpaloque; zan anhualcahcalactaque que' antiitzcuintotontin
did you give greetings; you came introducing yourselves like
  little dogs.

quen huelima niahuia,
Quen' huelimanniahuia,
What time is this right now when I am enjoying myself,

nipahqui, nicochi, cenca antecochizolohque;
nipahpaqui, 'huan nicochi? Cenca antecochzoloque;
when I am happy, and [when] I am sleeping? You have completely ruined [my] sleep;

cenca huel ante cochopahzolohque.
cenca huel antecochpahzoloque.
you have deeply troubled [my] sleep.

Nicno chicahua noyollo!
Nic-chicahua in noyollo![1]
I strengthen my heart [take courage]!

Maxihuala, tehuatl in ti, Cuahnahuacatl!
Ma xihuallauh, tehuatl in ti Cuahnahuacatl!
Come forward, thou of Cuernavaca!

tlein ipampa tinechtemohua?
Tlein ipampa in ti-nechtemohua?
Why dost thou come to seek me?

quemach huelima nican nicno-ilhuiquixtililia,
right now when I am here celebrating my *fiesta*.

quemach huelincuac nican nicno-ilhuitomililia
Quenmach hueli icuac nican nicno-[i]lhuitomililia
Is it possible [you come] right now when I am remembering

---

[1] *Nic-chicahua in noyollo.* The text is barbarous, influenced by the Spanish
construction. There is no necessity for the repetition in *nicno* and *noyollo.* The
exact translation of the text, as given above, is: "I fortify this heart of mine."
The classical poet would have agglutinated the expression thus: *Nino yol-chica-*

yehuatzin Ichpochtzintli Maliatzine
in yehuatzin Ichpochtzintli Maliaztin-e-e[1]
her the Virgin Holy Mary [who]

nican nechmomaquilihtica no-ayochicahuiliz[2]
nican nechmoyecmaquilihtica in noayochicahualiz
is here giving me fully my essential strength

ihuan no-ayotlahpalihuiz?
ihuan in no ayotlapalihuiz?
and my valor?

Mochicahua noyollo.
Nicchicahua in noyollo.
I strengthen my heart.

Maxihuala, tehuatl in ti, Yahtepecatl,
Maxihuallauh, tehuatl in ti Yahtepecatl!
Come forward, thou of Yautepec!

tlein ipampa tinechtemohua?
Tlein ipampa in ti nechtemohua,
Why dost thou seek me,

Ica hueloncan nechmoyohualotica
ca hueloncan nechmoyohualotica
[where] are surrounding me here

nahui notepe, chicome tlatelli, chicome tlacomolli,
nahui in notepe, in chicome tlahtlatelli, in chicome tlacomolli
my four mountains, the seven hills, the seven wells

---

hua ("I myself heart-fortify"); e.g., from the *Cantares mexicanos: Nino yol-
nonotza campa ni-cuiz yectli ahuiaca xochitl* ("I myself heart-consult—meditate—
where I shall gather beautiful-sweet-scented flowers").

[1] *Maliatzin-e-e:* The vocative *e*, pronounced long, often served as a complete
metric foot, thus *e-e.*

[2] *Ayo*, contraction for *ayotl*, the watery substance, the essence of anything.
Water, the gift of the Tlalocs, was essential for all vegetable growth; so *ayotl*
came to have the secondary meaning of "essential," which it has in the text.

ihuan chicome tlamimilolli;
'huan chicome tlaltemimilolli;[1]
and [the] seven stony hillsides;

no-ayochicahualiz ihuan no-ayotlahpalihuiz?
in no-ayochicaualiz 'huan no-ayotlapalihuiz?
they are my valor and my essential strength?

Nicnochicahua noyollo!
Nic-chicahua in noyollo!
I fortify my heart!

Maxihuala, tehuatl ti Tlayecapanecatl!
Ma xihuallauh in ti Tlayecapanecatl!
Come forward, thou of Tlayacapan!

tlein ipampa tinechtemohua?
Tlein ipampa in ti-nechtemohua?
Why dost thou seek me?

Cahuel nelli queh oquimohtlahui yehuatzin,
Ca-uel-nelli queh oquimo'talhui[2] *in yehuatzin,*
It is quite true as she, the aunt, said who shines

te ahuitzin, ompa ilhuicacxitoni,
te-ahuitzin,[3] *ompa ilhuicac-xitoni,*
there in the heavens,

---

[1] *Tlalte-mimilolli*, the rough, broken hill- or mountain-side; *tlaltetl*, "earth-stone," a ball of earth, clay, conglomerate, or volcanic matter found in abundance on the mountain slopes of the valley of Mexico; *mimiloa*, "to extend," "to increase," "to roll."

[2] *Mo'talhui; italhui*, "to speak," "to say," "to explain."

[3] *Te-ahuitzin*, the aunt (in general), substituted for *te-ci*, the aunt of one's grandparents. Teci was the ancestor of gods and men and the antecessor of Our Lady of Guadalupe at Tepeyac (Guadalupe). As the wife of the fire-god, in the older Mexican mythology, she was the goddess of birth and fertility and the ruler, like her husband, of the three divisions of the universe, the superterrestrial (all above the earth); the terrestrial (on the earth), and the subterrestrial (below the earth). Teci was the "hare in the moon" and, by metathesis, the moon herself, who assumed all the attributes of the goddess. When the grain was gathered in, the Mexican people held a great festival in (September) in honor of Teci (identified with the moon). The *Tepozteco* play seems to have been written to

metztli oquimoxopehpechtihtzino.
meztli oquimoxopechtihtzino.[1]
she, the moon, has made her dwelling [foundations].

matlactli ihuan ome cicitlaltin
Matlactli 'huan ome cicitlaltin
Twelve stars she has

oquimo xochi-icpacuiltitzino.
o-qui-mo-xoch'-icpac-cuiltitzino.
[like] flowers placed on her head.

omotlacempanahuilli ompa ilhuicac;
omotlacempanahuilli ompan in ilhuicac;
She has surpassed, there in the sky, all;

ihuan nican tlalticpac;
ihuan nican in tlalticpac;
and here on earth;

ihuan nohuiampa cemanahuac.
ihuan nohuiampa cemanahuac.
and everywhere in the universe.

Maxihuala, Tehuatl in ti-Huaxtepecatl!
Ma xihuallauh,[2] *tehuatl in ti, Huaxtepecatl*
Come forward, thou of Huaxtepec!

---

take the place of this old autumn festival. The reference in the text is to the old
heathen belief of the "old aunt" or ancestor, Teci, the moon, holding her court
in the sky, amid the stars. Teci was frequently identified with Chicome-xochitl
("Seven-Flowers"), the goddess of birth, who had her home among the stars.
This is probably the reference, in the text, to the seven flowers and the seven
stars. The Indians associated the Virgin with the moon.

[1] *Oquimoxopechtihtzino* (rev. form), "has made her foundation," that is, all
that lies beneath her, over which she rules or has dominion. *Xopechtli*, "foundation," is verbalized by the suffixing of *-tia*, "to make," and the prefixing of *mo*,
for "one's self." As verb it takes the objective pronoun *qui* = "has-it-for-herself-
foundation-made."

[2] *Ma xihuallauh*, imperative of *huallauh*, "to come toward." This word is
frequently written incorrectly because, in ordinary conversation, the *uh*-termina-
tion is not pronounced. This *-uh* formed one of the poetic licenses of the Aztec
poets, who pronounced it or not according to the necessities of the meter.

tlein ipampa tinechtemohua?
Tlein ipampa in ti-techtemohua?
Why dost thou seek me; at this

quemach huelima; quemach huilihcuac;
quemmach in huelimman; quemmach in huel-icuac;
very moment; just at this time;

nican nicno—ilhuiquixtililia;
nican nicno—[i]lhuiquixtililia;
is it possible—when I am celebrating my *fiesta;*

nican nicno-ilhuitomililia;
nican nicno'lhuitomililia;
when I am remembering the year-day;

nicnotlatlanamictililia nonantzin,
nicno tlahtlanamictililia in nonantzin,
when I am remembering my mother,

ichpochchichiltzintli ihuan
Ichpochchichitzintli ihuan
the roseate Virgin and

techalchi centeconetzin cencateoyotica,
te-chalchi-centeconetzin, cenca-yecteoyotica,
the precious only son, altogether divine,

yectililoni icatzinco in Teotl
in yectililoni icatzinco-[i]n Teotl
perfect as God

te-Tahtzin, in Teotl te-Piltzin ihuan in Teotl Teayotzin,
in te-Tatzin, Teotl in te-Piltzin, ihuan Teotl, te-Ihyotzin,
the Father, God the Son and God the Holy Ghost,

quemach omique ilhuicac ihuan nican tlalticpac,
quemmach-ami in ilhuicac ihuan nican in tlalticpac,
ever blessed in heaven and here on earth,

ihuan nicnohuian cemanahuactli.
ihuan icnohuian cemanahuac.
and also everywhere in the universe.

Nicnochicahua noyollo!
Nic-chicahua in noyollo!
I fortify my heart!

Maxihuala, ti Tlalmanacatl!
Ma xihuallauh, in ti Tlamanalcatl!
Come forward, thou from Tlalmanalco!

tlein ipampa tinechtemohua?
Tlein ipampa in ti-nech temohua?
Why dost thou seek me?

Maxihualacan, anmonochtin!
Ma xihualcan, anmo-nochtin!
Come forward, all of you!

xic-caquiqui tlein huel notenyo, notlahtol.
Xic-caqui-qui tlein-huel in notenyo, in notlahtol.[1]
Come to hear how great is my fame, my majesty.

Nepa ye huehca, canin anahuiaya anpahpactaya;
Nepa ye huecapa canin in an-ahahuia, an-pahpactiaya;
Far over there where you gloried [in your power];

[1] *Tenyo,* contraction of *tenyotl,* "fame": *tlatolli,* "word," and, in a secondary sense, "fame," "authority," "majesty." *N'amech,* "I from you"; *hual-anilit'on, anilia-tia,* "to cause to take or bring" (with *hual,* "toward"); *on,* "here, from there": "I have taken from you there and brought [them] here or caused them to be brought here, the *tlalpanhuehuetl* and the *tlalpanteponaztli.*" The former, as the war drum, which could be heard for five miles, was the symbol of national power and valor in battle; the latter was symbolical of the social side of life. It was the favorite musical instrument of the poets, song composers, and musicians of the courts of the kings of Mexico and Texcoco. The taking of these drums from the cities that made war on the Tepozteco symbolized their defeat in war and the disruption of their social life. The poem closes with the command of the Tepozteco to the court musicians to bring forth the war drum and beat the war music (with its accompanying war chant), thus proclaiming the victory of the Tepozteca and the humiliation of the warring cities. The *panhuehuetl* was a large upright drum; and the *tlal-panhuehuetl* was so called because it rested on the ground or floor.

The accentuation of words was somewhat different in the valley of Mexico from that of outlying Nahuatl territory. In the valley every word was accentuated on the penultimate; and the long compound words carried the accent regularly on every second syllable thereafter. This gave a succession of trochees and made the trochaic the natural Nahuatl meter.

canin amo centlamachtihtaya,
canin ammo [anmo]—centlamachtiaya,
where you had your pleasures; where you had your recreations,

amech hual anilihten anmotlalpanhuehuetl,
n'amech-hual-anilit'on anmo-tlalpanhuehuetl,
I took from you your war drum,

ihuan anmotlalteponaz.
ihuan anmotlalteponaz.
and your teponaztli.

Nicnochicahua noyollo!
Nic-chicahua in noyollo!
I fortify my heart!

Maxiquin hualtzotzonilican in pinahuiz!
Ma xi-quin-hualtzotzonilican in pinahuiz!
Beat for them [on the drum] their shame [of having been conquered]!

BIBLIOGRAPHY

ADAN, ELFEGO. "Las danzas de Coatetelco," *Anales del Museo Nacional de Arq., Hist. y Etn.*, XI (1910), 135–94.

ATL, DR. *Las artes populares en México*, Mexico: Librería "Cultura," 1921.

BANDELIER, ADOLPH F. *Report of an Archaeological Tour in Mexico in 1881*, "Papers of the Archaeological Institute of America, American Series," Vol. II. Boston, 1884.

BEALS, CARLETON. Article in *Mexican Life*, III, No. 3 (March, 1927).

BOAS, FRANZ. "Notes on Mexican Folk-Lore," *Journal of American Folk-Lore*, XXV (July–Sept., 1912), 204–60.

Book of Life of the Ancient Mexicans, The (publication of the Codex Magliabecchi, with translation of notes by T. T. Waterman). Berkeley: University of California Press, 1903.

BULNES, FRANCISCO. *The Whole Truth about Mexico: President Wilson's Responsibility*. New York: M. Bulnes Book Co., 1916.

CLAVIJERO, FRANCISCO J. *Historia antigua de Mexico*. Mexico: Departamento Editorial de la dirección general de las Bellas Artes, 1917.

COLBY, C. C. *Source Book for the Economic Geography of North America*. Chicago: University of Chicago Press, 1922.

COLIN, J. PAREDES. "Marriage Customs of San Juan Miautitlan," *Mexican Magazine*, III (May, 1927), 213–21.

Collección de documentos ineditos del Real Archivo de Indias. Madrid, 1869.

"The Coyote and the Opossum," *Mexican Folkways*, I, No. 2 (Aug.–Sept., 1925), 11.

CUSHING, SUMNER W. "The Distribution of Population in Mexico," *Geographical Review*, XI (1921), 227–42.

D'HARCOURT, R. ET M. *La musique des Incas et ses survivances*. Paris: Librairie Orientaliste, Paul Geuthner, 1925.

DÍAZ DEL CASTILLO, BERNAL. *A True History of the Conquest of New Spain* (translated into English by Alfred P. Maudslay). London: printed for the Hakluyt Society, 1908–16.

Dye, Alexander. "Railways and Revolutions in Mexico," *Foreign Affairs*, V, No. 2 (Jan., 1927), 320–21.

Espinosa, Aurelio M. "New-Mexican Spanish Folk-Lore," *Journal of American Folk-Lore*, XXIII (Oct.–Dec., 1910), 395–418.

Gennep, Arnold van. *Les rites de passage.* Paris: E. Nourry, 1909.

Gerste, A., S.J. *La médecine et la botanique des anciennes mexicaines.* Rome: Imprimerie Polyglotte Vaticaine, 1910.

González, Casanova P. "El cielo legendario del Tepoztecatl," *Revista mexicana de estudios historicos* (Mexico, 1928) II, 17–63.

González, Casanova P. "Un cuento Mexicano," *El Mexico antiguo*, I, Nos. 10–12, 291–307.

Gruening, Ernest. *Mexico and Its Heritage.* New York: Century Co., 1928.

Hernandez, Francisco. *Cuatro libros de la naturaleza y virtudes de las plantas de la Nueva España.* Edited by Peñafiel. Morelia, 1888. (First translated from Latin into Spanish and published in Mexico in 1615.)

Kroeber, A. L. Address delivered before the Social Science Research Council at Hanover, N.H., August 25, 1927 (unpublished).

Kroeber, A. L. "On the Principle of Order in Civilization as Exemplified by Changes of Fashion," *American Anthropologist* (N.S., 1919), XXI, 235–63.

Kroeber, A. L. "The Possibility of a Social Psychology," *American Journal of Sociology*, XXIII (1917), 633–50.

McBride, George McCutcheon. *Land Systems of Mexico*, "American Geographical Society, Research Series," No. 12. New York: American Geographical Society, 1923.

Malinowski, Bronislaw. Address under the title of "Anthropology as a Social Science" delivered before the Social Science Research Council at Hanover, N.H., August 10, 1926 (unpublished).

Mazari, Manuel. "Un antiguo padrón itinerario del estado de Morelos," *Memorias y revista de la Sociedad científica "Antonio Alzate,"* XLVIII, Nos. 1–6 (Jan.–June, 1927), 149–70.

Mena, Ramon. "El Zarape," *Anales del Museo Nacional de Arqueologia, Historia y Etnografía* (época 5a, Sept.–Oct., 1925), I, No. 4, 373–98.

de Mendizabal, M.O. "Powder That Kills and Powder That Amuses," *Mexican Folkways*, III (1927), 15.

Miranda y Marron, Manuel. "Una excursión a Tepoztlán, Morelos," *Memorias de la Sociedad Antonio Alzate*, XXIII, 19–42.

Novello, Roque J. Ceballos. *Guía para visitar las principales ruinas arqueologicas del estado de Morelos: Tepoztlán y Teopanzolco*, "Publicaciónes de la Secretaría de Educación publica," XXI, No. 3. Mexico, 1929.

Nuñez y Dominguez, José de. "The Alabado and Alabanzas," *Mexican Folkways*, II, No. 5 (Dec.–Jan., 1926), 12–17.

Nuñez y Dominguez, José de. *El Rebozo*. Mexico City: Departamento Editorial de la dirección general de las Bellas Artes, 1917.

Park, Robert E. "Migration and the Marginal Man," *American Journal of Sociology*, XXXIII, No. 6 (May, 1928), 881–93.

Porter, Katherine Anne. "Corridos," *Survey*, LII (May, 1924), 157–59.

Radcliffe-Brown, A. R. "The Methods of Ethnology and Social Anthropology," *South African Journal of Science*, XX (Oct., 1923), 124–47.

Radin, Paul. "Maya, Nahuatl and Tarascan Kinship Terms," *American Anthropologist* (N.S., Jan.–March, 1925), XXVII, No. 1, 101–2.

Redfield, Margaret Park. "Notes on the Cookery of Tepoztlán, Morelos", *American Journal of Folk-Lore*, XLII, No. 164 (April–June, 1929), 167–96.

Redfield, Robert. "The Calpolli-Barrio in a Present-Day Mexican Pueblo," *American Anthropologist* (N.S., April–June, 1928), XXX, No. 2, 282–94.

Redfield, Robert. "The Material Culture of Spanish-Indian Mexico," *ibid.* (N.S., Oct.–Dec., 1928), XXXI, No. 4, 602–18.

Redfield, Robert. "Remedial Plants of Tepoztlán: a Mexican Folk Herbal," *Journal of the Washington Academy of Sciences*, XVIII, No. 8 (April, 1928), 216–26.

ROBELO, CECILIO A. "Diccionario de Mitología Nahoa," *Anales del Museo Nacional de Mexico* (segunda época), V, 228–34.

RODRIGUEZ, FRANCISCO. "Descripción de la pyramide llamada Casa del Tepozteco, perteneciente al pueblo de Tepoztlán, Edo. de Morelos, etc.," *Proceedings of the International Congress of Americanists,* Mexico City, 1895.

ROJAS, MARIANO. *Manual de la lengua Nahuatl.* Mexico: José Donaciano Rojas, 1927.

SALINAS, MIGUEL. "La Sierra de Tepoztlán," *Memorias y revista de la Sociedad Científica "Antonio Alzate,"* XXXVIII, Nos. 9 and 10 (July, 1920), 355–85.

SELER, EDWARD. "Die Tempelpyramide von Tepoztlán," *Globus,* LXXIII, No. 8 (Feb., 1898), 123–29; reprinted as "The Temple Pyramid of Tepoztlán" in *Mexico and Central American Antiquities, Calendar Systems and History* (Bureau of American Ethnology), *Bull. 28,* pp. 339–52.

SILVA Y ACEVES, MARIANO. "La Colección folklorico de la biblioteca del Museo Nacional," *Anales del Museo Nacional* (época *5a,* July–Aug., 1925), I, No. 3, 269–320.

SMITH, J. RUSSELL. *North America.* New York: Harcourt, Brace & Co., 1925.

STARR, FREDERICK. "Notes on the Ethnography of Southern Mexico," *Proceedings of the Davenport Academy of Sciences,* Vol. VIII.

SUC, LOUIS. *Les plantes médicinales du Mexique.* Toulouse: Ch. Dirion, 1912.

THOMPSON, WALLACE. *The People of Mexico.* New York: Harper & Bros., 1921.

TOOR, FRANCES. "Cures and Medicine Women," *Mexican Folkways,* I, No. 2 (Aug.–Sept., 1925), 17–18.

TOOR, FRANCES. "Holy Week," *ibid.,* III, No. 1 (Feb.–March, 1927), 53–61.

TOOR, FRANCES. "I Am Cured of Fright," *ibid.,* II, No. 7 (June–July, 1926), 31–32.

TYLOR, EDWARD B. *Primitive Culture* (7th ed.). New York: Brentano's, 1924.

WATERMAN, T. T. *Bandelier's Contribution to the Study of Ancient Mexican Social Organization,* "University of California

Publications in American Archeology and Ethnology," XII, (1917), 249–82.

WISSLER, CLARK. *Man and Culture.* New York: Thomas Y. Crowell & Co., 1923.

WISSLER, CLARK. *The Relation of Nature to Man in Aboriginal America.* New York: Oxford University Press, 1926.

INDEX

INDEX